LANTERNS FOR THE DEAD

LANTERNS FOR THE DEAD

The Medieval *Lanternes des Morts*
of Central and South-West France

John Bate

LAPRIDGE PUBLICATIONS
1998

First published in 1998 by
Lapridge Publications
25 Church Street, Hereford HR1 2LR

ISBN 1 899290 05 2

British Library Cataloguing in Publication Data
A catalogue record for this book is available
from the British Library

Printed and bound in Great Britain by
Biddles Limited, Guildford and King's Lynn

TO RACHEL

CONTENTS

Contents   9

PREFACE

In 1863 an Irish antiquarian, Hodder Michael Westropp, while speculating on the origin of the round towers that are conspicuous features in the architecture of his country, made the suggestion that they might have derived their origin from the *fanaux de cimitières*, cemetery lanterns or lanterns for the dead that are to be found in certain cemeteries in France, raised as memorials to the dead, as beacons to guide funeral processions and to plead for the prayers of all those that passed by. In support of this theory he quoted at length from one of the earliest French descriptions of these *lanternes des morts*, that published in 1841 by the distinguished archaeologist Arcisse de Caumont, founder of the Société Française d'Archéologie. De Caumont's description, as given in translation by Westropp, is the first, and so far the only description of these monuments to appear in the English language. Its publication, as an obscure pamphlet, seems perhaps not surprisingly to have aroused no interest in England at that time: and during the 130 years that have followed, while French religious architecture has continued to be a subject of absorbing interest to many generations of antiquarians both professional and amateur in this country, these lesser but nonetheless intriguing monuments seem to have attracted no attention here.

Today, as the architectural treasures of France come to be appreciated by an ever-rising tide of visitors from Britain, among those treasures the *lanternes des morts* deserve to be recorded. I hope this account may aid those who discover them and provide something of what is known of their history including those that once stood and are no longer to be found.

ACKNOWLEDGEMENTS

The perceptive reader will appreciate the extent to which this work has depended on material gathered from libraries on both sides of the Channel. For this, among many others, I must thank the Society of Antiquaries of London, the Centre d'Études Supérieures de Civilisation Médiéval in Poitiers and many municipal libraries throughout central and south-west France, and especially those at Saintes and Limoges. For human resources my thanks go to Madame Gisèle Mazet of Felletin and Madame Arnauld of Saintes for welcoming me and for much valuable and knowledgeable help; and to Monsieur Gérard Dauxerre of Civray for his friendship and for sharing with me his considerable knowledge of the subject. Michael Olmert of the University of Maryland has taken a particular interest in *lanternes des morts* and I am sincerely grateful to him for his advice in the embryonic stages of the work and his salutary criticisms that have helped to shape it.

My very warmest thanks I offer to my friend Christian Gaumy of Limoges, a polymath and a most generous friend who, from the beginning has given me his help in ways too many and too varied to be adequately recorded here. To Paul Latcham I am most grateful for his guiding hand and his support and encouragement; and to my daughter Gillian for her generosity in lending me her expert help.

Except where otherwise indicated the photographs are my own.

INTRODUCTION

As enigmatic in their origin and intention as they are striking in appearance, the medieval *lanternes des morts* of central and south-west France are a small group of lesser religious monuments that have until lately remained little known outside antiquarian circles in their own country and all but unheard-of elsewhere. Their presence, often inconspicuous, in places sometimes far from the beaten track, partly accounts for this neglect; while cemeteries, in which many of them still stand, offer little to divert the passing traveller.

They are indeed cemetery lanterns as their name suggests, but to light the way for the steps of benighted visitors was not the object for which they were built. Their purpose was to display a votive light, dim and flickering as it must have been, as a living memorial to the dead whose mortal remains lay below in graves all too often nameless, an unspoken call to prayer for their souls and a reminder of mortality to the on-looker; expressions of the manifold symbolism of light that have come down from remote regions of antiquity. 'A beacon on the shore of eternity' was the lapidary epithet given to them by the nineteenth-century antiquarian Count Alexis de Chasteigner, author of the first comprehensive account of them, in 1843.

The traditional *lanterne des morts* is a free-standing tower of stone whose height may be from three up to twenty-two metres. It will have a hollow shaft, with an access door at or near the foot and a stone lantern at the top. It may rise directly from the ground, but more commonly from a more or less substantial stone base. It stands, or will once have stood, in a cemetery over which its light would have shone, distinguished from other forms of cemetery cross such as *croix hosannières* (Palm Sunday crosses) that have solid shafts and carry no lantern.

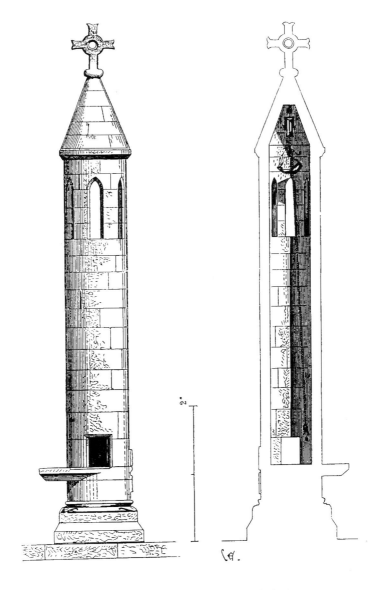

Anatomy of a *lanterne des morts*: Ciron (Indre)
(Viollet-le-Duc 1854–8)

There are some variations from this traditional pattern. The lantern may stand not on a free-standing column but on the roof or upper storey of a funeral chapel; it may be a feature of the structure of a church, in the form of a lantern-turret mounted on a buttress, a lighted window-opening, or a simple lamp-holding recess in one side of a buttress. Whatever their form, common to all the *lanternes des morts* is their location in or overlooking what was, and in some cases still is, a consecrated burial ground.

In traditional form or in one of its variants, some ninety-six *lanternes des morts* are known to have existed, and of these forty-eight are still standing. Many were lost during the years of revolution, many succumbed to age or in the cause of urban development. Many of the survivors owe their preservation to the interest taken in them by the Société Française d'Archéologie from its foundation by Arcisse de Caumont in 1834, and by provincial archaeologists and others throughout the nineteenth and twentieth centuries. By their efforts many lanterns that would otherwise have gone unrecorded were brought to light, and many were rescued from dereliction.

A fleeting custom

In the ecclesiastical history of France the construction and use of *lanternes des morts* occupy only a brief recorded span. They were built, with few exceptions, during the twelfth and thirteenth centuries; if there were precursors they have left no trace; perhaps through frailty of construction they did not long survive. Apart from the legend of the miraculous appearance of candelabra destined for the cemeteries at Vienne in AD 590 (p.134), the earliest evidence for the existence of such a monument (and the only account of its liturgical use) is an account given by Pierre-le-Vénérable, abbot of Cluny from 1122 to 1156. In his treatise '*de Miraculis*' he recounted the story, received from an older monk, of a nocturnal ceremony round a stone lantern raised above the cemetery of the abbey of Charlieu in Burgundy:

> *Obtinet autem medium cemeterii locum structura*
> *quaedam habens in summitate sui quantitatem unius*
> *lampadis capacem, quae ob reverentiam fidelium ibi*
> *quiescientium, totis noctibus fulgore suo, locum illum*
> *sacratum illustrat.*

> There stands in a central position in the cemetery a
> structure that has at its summit sufficient space for a
> single lamp which, out of reverence for the faithful at
> rest there, lights every night with its beams that holy
> place.

It is reasonable to suppose, from the respective ages of the
narrator and his informant, that this event took place either
very late in the eleventh century or very early in the twelfth,
showing that *lanternes des morts* and their ceremonial use were
already established by that time. Dates of foundation can be
suggested for very few of them and with little certainty; among
these the lantern at Sarlat (Dordogne) (p. 82) was, according
to tradition, founded to commemorate a visit by St. Bernard
in 1147; that at Mauriac (Cantal) (p. 121), presented to the
parish by the then curé, was endowed by him in 1268. Equally
definite is the date of 1225 for the foundation charter of the
lantern-bearing chapel at Fontevraud l'Abbaye (Maine-et-
Loire) (p. 46). Among the rest, the active existence during
the twelfth century of three more lanterns is attested to by
contemporary records of gifts for their maintenance; one in
Limousin, at Aureil, *c.* 1150 (p. 116); one in Aquitaine, at Dalon
in 1187 (p. 86) and one in Poitou, at Montazais in 1194
(p. 62). In the first half of the fourteenth century there are
records for the maintenance of cemetery lanterns in three
villages in the Forez mountains on the western edge of the
Rhône valley region (p. 132–3), and in 1399 the granting of a

charter for the erection of a cemetery chapel revealed the existence of a lantern in the cemetery of La Châtre in Berry (p. 39).

From then on, records cease. No more is heard of *lanternes des morts* until, in about 1620, Robert du Dorat, an early chronicler of Limousin, recorded the presence of several lantern-bearing obelisks and spires of stone in the Basse-Marche and Limousin, and told of a long-held tradition that glazed lanterns had been placed in them during the vigils of the great feast days, when the people, after keeping watch in the church, would resort to the cemetery to pray. He clearly implies that by his time these customs had long since ceased to be observed. And in 1685 Bonaventure de Saint-Amable in his *Histoire de Saint-Martial* (the apostle of the Limousin), gave an account of the *lanternes des morts* in the city of Limoges in which he referred specifically to their use in former times in the celebration of vigils.

Reasons for this decline in the devotional use of *lanternes des morts* remain obscure. Changes in religious thought and practice and in attitudes to death and the after-life may have contributed to it, as Plault (1988) has argued. But a no less effective physical influence must have been the chaos that accompanied and followed the recurrent passage of the Black Death from 1348 onwards, and the progress of the Hundred Years War. With plague victims dying in many places faster than the living could bury them, cemeteries must soon have become choked and would remain places to be avoided, under peril of death, perhaps for many years to come. Under such circumstances, and with a scarcity of priests to serve them, the continuance of pious observances beneath the light of a *lanterne des morts* would be impossible, and in many cases disuse must have led to permanent abandonment of such ceremonies, while the social and economic consequences of these calamities would have been anything but favourable to a revival.

Geographical distribution

Lanternes des morts are not widely dispersed across France; all but a few are confined within an area roughly bounded by the Loire on the north and east, the Dordogne on the south and the sea on the west. Within these bounds the greatest number are concentrated in the Limousin region, whose present-day boundaries correspond almost exactly with those of the medieval diocese of Limoges. The number of lanterns in and around the cathedral city (no fewer than five once existed in the city itself) points to this as the cradle of the lantern-building movement which was to extend in a relatively short time across central and south-west France. From this focus in Limousin, lantern-building spread westward into what are now the regions of Poitou-Charentes and Aquitaine and eastward into Auvergne. Small numbers appeared in regions adjoining these on the north and there are, or once were, isolated outliers as far away as Montmajour in Provence, Avallon in Burgundy and in Paris.

No explanation has been found for this proliferation of *lanternes des morts* within a relatively well-defined area and their absence elsewhere in the country. The destructive forces of war, of civil strife and of disease cannot be held to account for the absence of lanterns in other parts of the country since these forces were no less active in areas where *lanternes des morts* are or once were to be found. Their distribution bears no relation to any of the great pilgrimage routes. The suggestion that one or other of the monastic orders might have promoted their building was investigated by Crozet (1943:126). His analysis showed that while parishes having *lanternes des morts* were more likely to be affiliated to Benedictine establishments than to those of other orders, this predominance was not significant when set against the general prevalence of Benedictines over other orders. He also pointed to similar anomalies of geographical distribution in other parts of the country, such as the localisation of elaborately sculptured

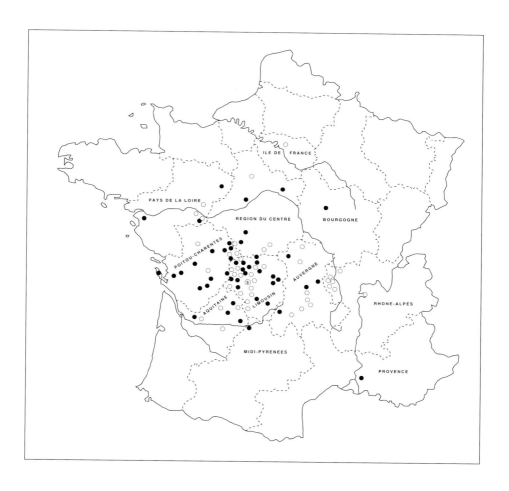

Geographical distribution of *lanternes des morts* in France
Existing *lanternes* ●   *Lanternes* lost ○

ossuaries and calvaries in Brittany, of roadside oratories in Provence and of *armoires eucharistiques* (aumbries with external windows, often lighted, for the display of the consecrated elements of the holy sacrament) in eastern France.

Funerary lanterns are not confined to France. A large number are known in Austria, Germany and elsewhere in Central Europe. They have been surveyed by the Austrian archaeologist the late Franz Hula, whose map (p. 22) shows their distribution. They differ from their French counterparts in their post-medieval origin and in their architectural features; pillar lanterns, wall lanterns, niches and oculi far outnumber free-standing towers on the French pattern. A small number of French lanterns, in Alsace, Lorraine and Franche-Comté, belong more properly, on architectural grounds and by date, to the Central European group and are not included here. One lantern is recorded in Italy; built in about 1300 over a funerary chapel at the Cistercian abbey of San Galgano near Siena, it no longer exists.

The round towers resembling *lanternes des morts*, of which over one hundred are recorded in Ireland, together with two in Scotland and one in the Isle of Man, differ in date, in structure and in purpose from *lanternes des morts*. Built for the most part in the tenth and eleventh centuries, they are of an earlier generation. Although their religious significance is evident from their location in ecclesiastical sites as well as by tradition, nevertheless it is also clear that for many of them their structure shows that their prime purpose was defensive rather than reverential; the protection of their monastic occupants and their treasures against the depredations of Viking raiders. Though outwardly resembling *lanternes des morts*, they are generally on a much larger scale (up to 34m high and 6m in diameter at the base, with walls up to 1.2m thick surrounding a central cavity from 2m to 3m wide). The central cavity was usually subdivided by a succession of floors for living space and storage. Entrance was by a door raised well clear of the ground, reached by a ladder that could be drawn up inside when needed to deter invaders. Lantern windows at the top provided a look-out post by day and a beacon at night. The two towers in Scotland, at Abernethy in Perthshire and at Brechin in Angus, and that at Peel in the Isle of Man, were built to a similar plan and are thought to have served the same purposes as the Irish round towers. (Westropp 1863; Edwards 1990: 127–8).

Ritual purposes

The twelfth-, thirteenth- and fourteenth-century records of gifts for the maintenance of cemetery lanterns leave no doubt about the pious intention of *lanternes des morts* at those times and in those places. Thus, in Aquitaine:

> … *pour rappeler à la destruction de son enveloppe de chair, en 1167 Guillaume de Tournon avait donné six livres qu'on devait employer à entretenir pendant la nuit un luminaire dans la cimetière de Dalon.*

> … to remind all that the soul survives the destruction of its covering of flesh, in 1187 Guillaume de Tournon gave six pounds to be used for the maintenance during the night of a lamp in the cemetery at Dalon.

Endowments with the same intent were provided at Montferrand in Auvergne, Montsoreau in the western Loire Valley as well as those already mentioned, at Aureil in Limousin and at Montazais in Poitou. Recognition of the pious intention of *lanternes des morts* was preserved in Limousin well into the seventeenth century, witnessed as we have seen by the chronicler Robert du Dorat.

But this intention was by no means always or universally admitted. The five hundred years that were to pass between the time of their building and their recognition and

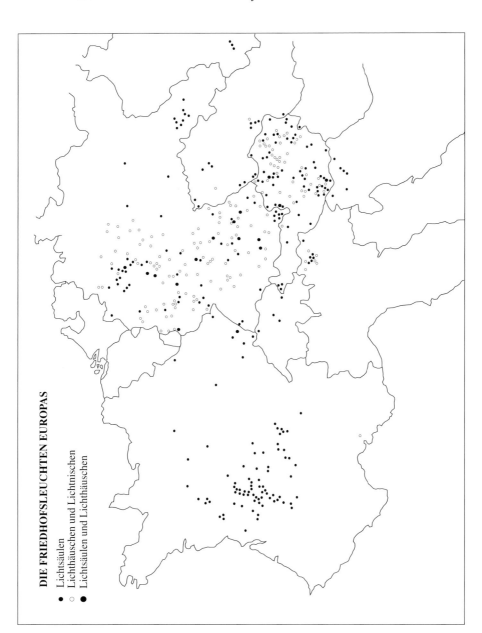

DIE FRIEDHOFSLEUCHTEN EUROPAS

Lichtsäulen
Lichthäuschen und Lichtnischen
Lichtsäulen und Lichthäuschen

● ○ ●

Geographical distribution of cemetery lanterns in Europe (Hula 1971)

systematic study in the late eighteenth and nineteenth centuries provided fertile ground for the proliferation of legend and superstition. René Crozet (1943) listed some of the more bizarre suggestions:

> For certain authors *lanternes des morts* were beacons to guide weary travellers or to indicate cemeteries from afar off, either to find them more easily, or, on the contrary, to avoid them. For others they would have shed light on the meetings between relatives of the dead; beneath their light, women gave themselves to religious and mystical dances; in epidemics they were a source of light; they would allow the dead who had left their tombs by night to find them again before dawn.

Among serious authors, in 1729 Dom Jean Mabillon, historian of the Benedictine order, paid little attention to the reverential intent of the two lanterns he had seen, at Sarlat in the Dordogne and Bonneval (Eure-et-Loir), considering only their utility, declaring that their light was intended only for the benefit of those attending church by night: '... *illuminandos eos qui ad ecclesiam noctu conveniebant.*' In 1792 Dom Bernard Montfaucon, in the Supplement to his monumental *Livre de l'antiquité expliquée*, attributed a pre-Christian origin to the five lanterns he described, regarding them as pagan temples of Gaulish origin. And when confronted with the lantern-tower dedicated to *Notre-Dame-des-Bois* in the cemetery of the Holy Innocents in Paris, he found himself unable to decide whether it was a watch-tower or an aid to navigation on the Seine. The views of Montfaucon were echoed by the later eighteenth-century writers Piganiol de la Force (1742: 304) and the Abbé Expilly (1762: 44). Not until the early years of the nineteenth century was recognition of the true intention of *lanternes des morts* restored by numerous writers less exalted but with the advantage of being indigenous; Allou (1821: 164) in Limousin, Bouillet (1834: 338) in Auvergne and others, with de Caumont (1837: 428) and most notably de Chasteigner, whose 1843 review covered most aspects of the subject, as well as providing descriptions of twenty-one lanterns known up to that time.

From then on it may be said to have become generally accepted that the lantern light, a symbol of life descended from the remotest pagan past, was a living memorial to the dead and an unspoken invocation to prayer for their souls. There were also adventitious uses; the lanterns would have served as landmarks for benighted travellers or for funeral processions coming from afar; distances between cemeteries were often very great, and it could happen that after a long journey, perhaps of several days, a corpse might be in no fit state to enter a church; the light of the lantern would ensure that the deceased so excluded would not be bereft of the light of a funerary candle. The lantern might give warning of the proximity of a cemetery with the fear of infection or of ghostly visitation. A prosaic legend had it that the lantern tower in the cemetery at Parigné-l'Evêque near Le Mans was built by the English and used as a beacon to guide their troops on night exercises during their occupation of Maine between the eleventh and fifteenth centuries (Étoc-Demazy 1841: 352). The opinion of today is concisely expressed by the sign erected beside the lantern at Coussac-Bonneval (Haute-Vienne):

Honneur rendu aux morts, avertissement donné aux vivants, point de repère du voyageur égaré dans la nuit, la lanterne des morts répond à ce triple but.

Honour paid to the dead, warning given to the living, a landmark for the traveller astray in the night, the lantern for the dead fulfils this threefold purpose.

Implicit in these expressions of intent is the recognition

that, above all, these memorials were collective in their purpose rather than individual, commemorative of all those buried within the consecrated ground; they were built in an age when most graves were unmarked and for only the greatest could there be a memorial within the church. For those of lesser rank there might be interment *sub stillicidio* (aspersed by the sanctified raindrops that fell from the eaves of the church) but for the great majority the *lanterne des morts* with its age-old symbolism was their only memorial.

Ritual practices

Little is known about the times during which the lanterns would have burned, but from Pierre-le-Vénérable, and from the deeds of gift already referred to, it is known that at Charlieu and at Dalon the lantern burned every night, and at Mauriac every Saturday night. The lanterns spoken of by Robert du Dorat in Limousin were lit on special occasions such as the nights of All Souls and All Saints, Good Friday and the festival of St. Peter's Chains (August 1st). The lantern at Parthenay-le-Vieux was endowed, unusually, to burn not only every night but every day as well. For the great majority there is no evidence of the practices they followed. While some parishes may have lit their lamps as often and as regularly as those quoted, the ability to do so would depend on the funds available for the supply of oil, and some, at times unable to meet this communal responsibility, may have had to restrict themselves to vigils and funeral occasions. In Limousin, at Saint-Amand-Magnazeix and Saint-Barbant, groves of walnut trees were planted to provide oil; at Saint-Goussaud it was paid for by public subscription; at Le Falgoux in Auvergne it was a responsibility accepted by certain families in the district, passed on by inheritance. At Les Moutiers-en-Retz in the western Loire Valley, the practice of lighting the lamp on the death of a parishioner, to burn until after the funeral, has continued to this day with the benefit of electricity, which enables also the nightly illumination of the lantern at La Souterraine in Limousin.

In places where the cemetery had no separate cross, the *lanterne des morts*, might be used, decked with consecrated greenery as a *croix hosannière* at the centre of the Palm Sunday celebrations; such a use is recorded at Parthenay-le-Vieux (p. 53) and other places. Occasionally a lantern so used might receive a distinctive cognomen; at Fenioux *Croix de Lousanne*; at Cellefrouin *Croisonnière*.

Varieties of structure

Of those free-standing towers that survive, sixteen are round, as at Château-Larcher (p. 56), seven are square as at Antigny (p. 56), seven polygonal as at Saint-Pierre d'Oléron (p. 69), and two are made up of clustered columns as at Fenioux (p. 64). The tallest is that at Saint-Pierre d'Oléron, 22 metres, the shortest, at 3.50 metres, at Estivareilles (p. 121). Though a small number rise straight out of the ground, most of them stand on a more or less substantial stepped base. The hollow interior, with a doorway at the foot, gives access to the lantern at the top by means of a spiral stair, by footholds cut in the wall or by the rock-climber's method, using counter-pressure on the back and the feet. In some cases the size of the entrance leads one to suspect that children were used as lamplighters, but where the diameter of the shaft would be insufficient even for that, the lamp could be raised by chain and pulley. The outline of the lantern chamber usually continues that of the shaft; square and polygonal lanterns have an opening on each wall; circular and clustered-column towers may have as few as three or as many as thirteen openings. Roofs are of stone, conical, pyramidal or bell-shaped, with a cross of stone or iron at the apex.

Twelve lanterns have a stone table, either cantilevered out from the shaft or supported on a pillar or a block of stone, about one metre above the base. These are invariably on the west side of the monument so that a priest officiating there at a funeral rite would face eastwards. The question of what ceremonies these tables were intended to serve has never been answered. Although liturgically oriented, their small size (with one exception, at Saint-Pierre d'Oléron), inconvenient position and exposure to the elements make it unlikely that they were used for the celebration of masses, as was suggested by Murcier (1855: 146) and others. Lacroix (1873: 529) went so far as to declare unequivocally that they could not have been consecrated altars, since celebration of mass in the open air was not allowed in those times, and Crozet (1943: 122) confirmed that no record of a mass celebrated at a *lanterne des morts* had ever been found. It seems more probable that these small tables were mainly intended to hold gospels, psalters and other devotional books needed in the course of an interment. The fact that one of the tables, at Estivareilles (p. 121), is inclined and forms a lectern gives some support to this view.

A stone stoup for holy water appears in two places; at Les Moutiers-en-Retz (p. 46) it stands out from the left-hand side of the stone table; and at Fenioux (p. 64) a bowl has been excavated in the top of the plinth at the south-west corner.

Of the two surviving lanterns built over funerary chapels, one, at Fontevraud-l'Abbaye (p. 46), is a slender octagonal tower rising from the apex of the chapel roof; the other, at Sarlat (p. 82), is a drum-shaped upper storey over the round chapel below.

Those lanterns or lantern-bearing recesses that form part of the structure of a church show some diversity of form. The simplest are mere niches in the wall of a church or in a buttress overlooking the churchyard as at Naves (p. 91). Others are oculi or windows through which the light of a lamp could shine from inside the building, as at Razès (p. 110); or a lantern-turret may stand on the top of a buttress as at Saint-Junien (p. 113). Very rarely a short solid pillar replaces the hollow column, as at Mauriac (p. 121).

Summary

Ninety-six medieval *lanternes des morts* are listed in this survey. Forty-eight still exist, most of them still intact, though not necessarily occupying their original sites. Of these, thirty are, or once were, free-standing towers, two are pillar-lanterns, seven are based on funerary chapels and nine form part of a church building. Of those that have disappeared, the record, which can only be conjectural, shows thirty-eight free-standing or not otherwise described, two pillar-lanterns, seven based on funerary chapels and one occupying a buttress against the wall of a church.

THE *LANTERNES*

Entries for existing *lanternes* are given in Roman type;
those that have disappeared are in italics.

ÎLE DE FRANCE

PARIS Cemetery of the Holy Innocents

*The cemetery of the church of the Holy Innocents was a piece of
land on the right bank of the Seine set apart as a burial ground
by Philippe Auguste at a time when the rapidly growing city
urgently needed more space for the burial of its dead. The cemetery extended westwards from the rue Saint-Denis between the
rue de la Ferronnerie on the south and the rue aux Fers (now the
rue Berger) on the north. At its eastern end stood the church, its
west front facing the cemetery. In a general view of the cemetery
and its surroundings (p. 32) the* lanterne des morts *can be seen
standing a little apart from the south-west corner of the church
and separated from it by an incongruous four-storey building,
apparently a house. Three funeral processions are proceeding in
the middle distance.*

*Eighteenth-century descriptions agree that the lantern tower,
thought to date from the late twelfth century, was octagonal and
about 40 feet high, whose lowest storey, the funerary chapel dedicated to Notre-Dame-des-Bois, eventually became buried to a
depth of 18 feet under 500 years of cemetery debris. The lowest
storey remaining above ground had a diameter of 12 feet; it contained the spiral staircase leading up to the octagonal lantern.*

*It was estimated that, during its six-hundred-year existence,
more than two million corpses were interred in the cemetery. By
the time that it was closed by decree of the Conseil d'État in
1785, it had become a scene of indescribable filth and corrup-
tion. It is supposed that the Tour Notre-Dame-des-Bois was
demolished soon afterwards, when the ground was cleared to
become a market. Today the site has become the Square des
Innocents.*

(Lebeuf 1754: 50–1; de Montfaucon 1757: 144–5; Lacroix 1873: 529)

VUE de L'ÉGLISE et du CIMETIERE des SS. INNOCENTS.

Paris: the church and cemetery of the Holy Innocents
(J-M-B de Saint-Victor, *Tableau historique et pittoresque de Paris*,
atlas, 2nd edn., 1822, pl. 85. © cliché Bibliothèque d'art et
d'archéologie Jacques Doucet, Paris)

Paris: Tour Notre-Dame-des-Bois (de Montfaucon 1757)

TOUR OCTOGONE DU CIMETIERE DES INNOCENS
DE PARIS

LIV. *Pl. du Tom. IV.*

Tom. IV. 54.

Paris: Tour Notre-Dame-des-Bois. A later state; the shrine is a
contemporary accretion. (Lenoir 1867)

LOIRE VALLEY - CENTRE REGION

Eure-et-Loir

BONNEVAL
10km N of Châteaudun

Dom Jean Mabillon, historian of the Benedictine order, reported having seen here a tower beside the church that resembled the lantern tower that he had seen at Sarlat in Aquitaine (p. 82). There is no other record of such a tower at Bonneval, and there is no trace of it in a town plan dated 1654, so that its authenticity as a lanterne des morts *must be considered doubtful.* (Mabillon 1729: 6.381; Sidoisne 1931: 219–20)

Indre

CIRON
14.5km E of Le Blanc N151

Facing on to a lane (D44) running south from the village, the *lanterne des morts* stands, on the site of a vast abandoned medieval cemetery, on a wide square plinth with eight full-width steps on the west side. (The steps on the other three sides were removed in 1760 by the then curé to be used in building a new sacristy for the church.) The slender cylindrical column of grey limestone 7.20m high, 0.80m in diameter is surrounded at the base by a torus on a square slab. The lantern chamber has six narrow lancet windows beneath a conical stone roof carved with downward-pointing serrations.

An incongruous pineapple finial replaces the cross which was knocked off during the Revolution. A south-facing doorway 0.30m x 0.80m leads to the smooth-walled interior of the shaft; there are no footholds and no means of raising the lamp can be seen. A weathered stone table 0.80m x 0.50m projects westwards at the level of the foot of the door, 1.00m above the base; on the opposite side of the column a broken-off

Ciron (Indre)

stump is thought to be the remains of either a credence or a holy-water stoup. Angle-spurs extend from the torus at the foot of the column to the angles of the basal slab, and these, together with the lancet windows, are considered to indicate a late twelfth- or early thirteenth-century origin.
(de la Villegille 1840: 10–12; Hubert, E. 1889: 115–16)

ESTRÉES-SAINT-GENOU   26km NW of Châteauroux
N143

This rugged lantern tower stands alone just off the side road to Saint Genou (D63B) in a meadow with wide views over the Indre valley where its light would be visible from afar. The meadow was formerly the cemetery of the now ruined Benedictine monastery in the town of Saint-Genou. After the closure of the cemetery the ground was dug over and large amounts of stone extracted, lowering the level of the ground and exposing, as can be seen, the foundations of the lantern tower. When first described, in 1840, it was in a seriously dilapidated state, in which it was to remain until 1870, when it was rescued by the Société Française d'Archéologie.

The restored column, 8.30m high, has its lower half encased in an octagonal sheath of smoothly dressed limestone blocks which form a truncated cone tapering to the girth of the upper half of the shaft. This, by contrast, is of roughly coursed much weathered stone with deeply eroded joints. It has a diameter of approximately 1.20m. The lantern chamber has three vertical openings with a dripstone below; above, a circular slab with a central hole covers in the shaft and supports a diminutive cone bearing the remains of an iron cross. A round-headed doorway 1.50m high, standing 0.50m above the present ground level and facing south-south-west, leads to the interior of the shaft, where no obvious means of ascent can now be seen. There are no features that would enable a date to be given to this artless monument.
(de la Villegille 1840: 7–10; Hubert, E. 1889: 114–15)

Estrées-Saint-Genou (Indre)

AIGURANDE 26km SW of La Châtre

First mentioned, in passing, by the antiquary Dom Bernard de Montfaucon in 1724 as an octagonal temple of Gaulish origin, this tower was described in some detail, though still in ignorance of its purpose, by Piganiol de la Force, thirty years later. It was an octagonal structure 20–25 feet in height, standing on an octagonal plinth, hollow within and having a small window on each face. There was a low door at the foot and above it a stone slab, thought to be an altar. The dome that covered in the shaft was smoke-blackened. Piganiol remarked on the excellent state of preservation of the monument in comparison with that of the similar monument that he had seen in the cemetery of the Holy Innocents' church in Paris (p. 31).

In the parish archives was a document in which it was laid down that the curé was 'to keep a light burning at the top of the cemetery lantern' from the 27th to the 29th of October, the feast of Saint Simon and Saint Jude, on which occasion he was to hold a service for the seigneurs of Aigurande and to recite a libera *over the tombs and monuments of deceased seigneurs.*

The lantern survived the closure of the cemetery in 1779, but after years of popular efforts to preserve it, its overthrow was decreed in secret by revolutionary iconoclasts and carried out under cover of darkness and with official complicity on the night of 30–31 May 1795.
(Pierre 1934: 35–40)

LA CHÂTRE 36km SE of Châteauroux

Known from a charter of 1399 granted to a citizen, Hugues Biard, to build a funerary chapel in the cemetery there 'prope et juxta lampadarum dicti cimiterii' *(hard by the lantern of the said cemetery). This lantern was said to be 'a beacon or lantern raised up on a platform of ten steps, constructed on the model of that at Arras' (the pyramid of the Holy Candle commemorating miraculous cures of the burning sickness by drops of its wax mixed*

*with water, in about 1200). The cemetery was closed in 1784
and the lantern destroyed with it.*
(Hubert, E. 1889: 109–16; Huignard 1936: 174)

SAINT-HILAIRE-SUR-BENAIZE   19km S of Le Blanc
*In a meadow that had formerly been a cemetery, a lantern said
to have resembled that at Ciron (p. 35). After closure of the
cemetery the lantern had regularly been the destination of Corpus Christi processions until, in 1833 or 1834, the owner of the
meadow had it pulled down.*
(de la Villegille 1840: 13)

Loir-et-Cher

RHODON   19km ESE of Vendôme D17 D69
A hexagonal turret, approximately 13m high, arising at the
south-west corner of the nave of the thirteenth-century church
of Saint-Cloud. The lantern has six tall, pointed arches that
have been walled up to the level of the imposts, presumably
to maintain stability. A spiral stair ascends to it from an internal doorway in the south wall at the west end of the nave.
This is kept firmly closed and warning notices forbid further
investigation.

It must be added that the interior of the church is of great
interest; in particular the roof, a succession of diagonal rib-
vaults whose supporting columns have variously decorated
capitals. The walls and the vaults are entirely covered with
thirteenth- and fifteenth-century paintings of scenes and figures from the New Testament. But on many of these the
ravages of damp are all too evident.
(Enlart 1902: 798)

Rhodon (Loir-et-Cher): lantern-turret at the south-west corner of the church of Saint-Cloud

Loiret

GERMIGNY-DES-PRÉS   28km E of Orléans N460 D60
The square lamp-chamber of a sixteenth- or seventeenth-century cemetery lamp set up on a pillar in the church enclosure. Its ball-finial now carries an iron weathercock on a long stem.
(Hubert, J. 1930: 534)

Germigny-des-Prés (Loiret)

LOIRE VALLEY - WEST REGION

Sarthe

PARIGNÉ-L'EVÊQUE   16km SE of Le Mans D304

The *lanterne des morts* stands on a slight eminence in the cemetery on the north-east side of the town, a conspicuous landmark over a wide stretch of open country. The striking and solitary appearance the lantern must once have shown has been much diminished by the funerary chapel of Notre-Dame de la Pitié, now derelict, which was built up against its south side in the fifteenth century.

The column is cylindrical, 13.00m high, standing on a circular base of three steps. Its diameter at mid-height is approximately 2.00m; above this level a slight upward taper is evident. It is built of random rubble, rendered in places; the four narrow round-headed windows that form the lantern are of blocks of dressed stone. The lantern is overhung by the eave of the conical roof of tufa, which rises in a graceful curve to support the stone cross. A low rectangular doorway opens into the shaft at the foot on the north side; inside, fourteen footholds on either side make for a hazardous ascent to the summit where a bell and an electric lamp now hang. Nothing is known about the history of the lantern, which dates from the twelfth century; local tradition attributes its building to the English during their occupation of Maine from the twelfth to the fifteenth century.

(Étoc-Demazy 1841: 349–53)

Parigné-l'Evêque (Sarthe)

Loire-Atlantique

LES MOUTIERS-EN-RETZ 47km SW of Nantes D751 D758 D13

In a public garden, formerly the cemetery, on the north side of the church, a cylindrical ashlar column 7.50m high, 1.25m in diameter. There are three rectangular glazed windows below a domed roof bearing a stone cross. On the west side is a solid stone table; from its north side an ancient stoup is corbelled out. Above the table is a recess containing a statue of St. Joseph, patron saint of all who desire a peaceful death. On the north side three steps lead to a doorway; inside eight steps lead up to a lamp platform. The present building dates only from 1887; it was originally built in the twelfth century and rebuilt for the first time in 1610. Now electrically lit, the lantern still fulfils its purpose; the parish of Les Moutiers is one of the few places where during the nights between the death of a parishioner and the interment, as well as on the feast of All Souls, the light still shines.
(Lecler 1882: 80–1; Boutin 1975: 63–4).

Maine-et-Loire

FONTEVRAUD-L'ABBAYE 14km SE of Saumur D974

The chapel of Ste-Catherine (of Alexandria) stands to one side of a tree-lined lane leading west from the parish church. It is outside the precincts of the abbey in ground, now partly built over, that was once the parish cemetery. Its foundation by Ala, duchess of Bourbon, a *réligieuse* of the abbey, is confirmed by a charter of 1225 that includes provision for the maintenance of a light. It is a square building with a pyramidal roof of stone, each corner embraced by a square buttress capped by a pyramid. An octagonal lantern tower 5.00m high

Les Moutiers-en-Retz (Loire-Atlantique)

Fontevraud-l'Abbaye (Maine-et-Loire): Chapelle Sainte-Catherine

rises from the apex of the roof; its windows, one on each face, have trefoil heads and there is a square access opening at the foot of the column on the south side. The original lantern tower was taken down and rebuilt in the fifteenth century, and was again rebuilt in the course of a general restoration of the chapel in 1960–2.

The funerary chapel is square in plan with sides of 8m, and stands over a vaulted crypt, now inaccessible. On each of three sides is a round-headed window, and on the fourth (west) side an entrance door. Internally an arcade of eight pointed arches encloses the windows and door and spans the corners. The arches spring from sculptured corbels at slightly above mid-height of the walls. From the angles of the octagon so formed and from the sculptured keystones there arise sixteen ribs that converge to unite at the apex of the vault in a torus that forms an oculus opening into the lantern tower. The buttress embracing the south-west corner contains a spiral stair leading down to the crypt and up to the roof for access to the lantern. The entrance to this has been walled up.

After many vicissitudes (at one time it was used as the *mairie* and later became a barn) the chapel has been for some years in the sympathetic hands of a Parisian architect who has restored it and now leases it to the local *Syndicat d'Initiative* as a tourist information office, open to the public during the season.

(Martin 1841: 540–44).

MONTSOREAU   11km E of Saumur

First mentioned in an anonymous text Considérations et Pratiques de Piété *published at Château-Gontier in 1716:* 'A similar beacon exists in the cemetery of Montsoreau in Anjou ...' *(Négrier 1858). Its existence was confirmed and its destruction recorded in 1878:* 'In the cemetery which adjoins the church there could be seen, until recently, one of those curious lanterns

*or beacons for the dead, almost unique in Anjou in our time,
and which someone was pleased to knock down without even
the pretext of making use of the stone (1865).'*
(Port 1878: 733–4)

MOULIHERNE   26km N of Saumur

*This lantern was described at some length in the anonymous text
of 1716 referred to above. It was a round tower of tufa, surrounded by six engaged colonnettes, about fifteen feet high with
an internal diameter of two feet. At the top were six small lantern windows beneath a dome vault carrying a stone cross;
beneath was a hole, presumably intended to contain a hook for
suspension of the lamp. There was an access door at the foot on
the north side. The tower stood on a mound that covered a
vaulted crypt with a holy-water stoup on one wall. To the west
of the tower stood an ornate stone table with a cross, where the
gospel was read on Palm Sunday. Stone steps on all sides except
the east gave access to the top of the mound. The tower was
destroyed in 1793. An unsympathetic modern replacement was
erected on the former site in 1978.*
(Négrier 1858: 11; Port 1878: 756)

SAUMUR (Saint-Nicolas)

*A funerary chapel surmounted by a lantern-tower on the site of
the former cemetery of the church of Saint-Nicolas in the centre
of the town. Believed to date from the end of the thirteenth century, the chapel is said to have resembled that at Fontevraud-
l'Abbaye; the lantern-tower above it was a tall eight-sided pyramid rising to a height of twelve metres above ground level; the
lantern windows are not shown in any existing illustrations.
When first described, in 1862 on the occasion of a meeting of the
Congrès archéologique de France in Saumur, the monument was
already engulfed in surrounding buildings, the cemetery having
been closed and the land redeveloped. Over the succeeding years*

it has, against strong local opposition, been allowed to disintegrate, its classification as monument historique *has been withdrawn and no trace of it can now be found.*
(de Verneilh 1862: 259–61; Girouard 1936: 21–3)

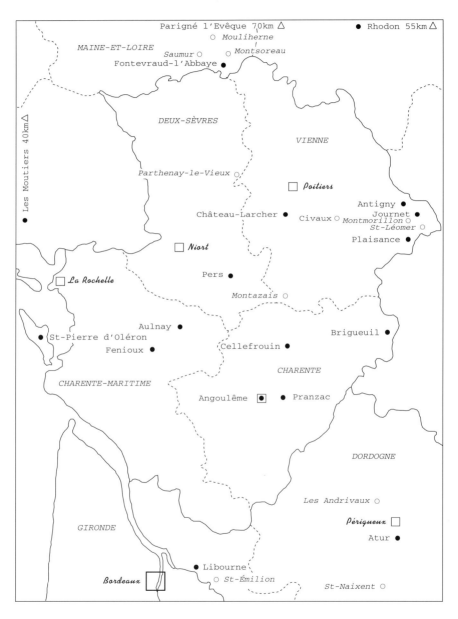

Poitou-Charentes with parts of adjacent regions
Approximate sites of *lanternes des morts*   existing ●   lost ○
Principal towns ☐

POITOU-CHARENTES

Deux Sèvres

PERS   **47km SE of Niort D948 D110**
This small and elegant lantern-tower stands in a well-kept
grass-grown cemetery in pastoral surroundings where nineteenth-century ironwork has given way to an array of
Merovingian tombs. Standing on a square plinth in the centre of a circular lawn raised two steps above the general level,
it rises to a height of 7.10m, a slender cylindrical shaft 0.68m
in diameter between four engaged colonnettes. These rise to
capitals ornamented with leaf and ball-flower crockets, and
continue upwards to unite at the apex of the steeply pitched
conical roof between a square block that carries the cross.
The lantern consists of four narrow round-headed windows
facing the cardinal points. At the foot of the shaft on the
north side a doorway 1.05m high, 0.27m wide opens into the
interior, where the wall has evenly spaced notches for climbing. From the west face a stone table 0.67m by 0.45m is
cantilevered out 1.10m above the top of the plinth. Late
thirteenth century.
(Berthelé 1889: 489)

PARTHENAY-LE-VIEUX   **1km S of Parthenay**
*Said to have been an octagonal lantern standing in the cemetery
on a hollow column raised on eight circular steps. Unusually, its
light was to burn by day as well as by night, for which a fund was
established to provide three hundred litres of oil yearly. Destroyed in 1792, it was known locally as the* croix hosannière
*because on Palm Sunday the gospel was read there and leafy
branches tied to the cross.*
(Briquet 1840: 213)

Pers (Deux Sèvres)

Pers: the lantern

Vienne

ANTIGNY   **15km N of Montmorillon D5 D33**
The old cemetery, once part of a vast Gallo-Roman necropolis and now the unencumbered village green, slopes down to
the main street, enclosed by a double row of pleached trees
that form a frame for the square column of the *lanterne des
morts*. This stands in a central position looking across to the
twelfth-century church, which has interesting wall-paintings.
When first described in 1841, it was standing in the south-
east corner of the cemetery, in an area paved with the broken
remains of sarcophagi. In 1880 it was taken down, the stones
being numbered, and re-erected on its present site.

It is a square limestone tower standing on a rectangular
plinth 1.30m high on a square four-stepped base from which
it rises to a height of 7.00m, with sides of 0.90m. The angles
are ornamented with fine colonnettes that rise from diminutive claws at the foot to crocketed capitals below the pyramidal roof. The four lantern windows are rectangular, with
rebated sides. On the west side the plinth supports a stone
table 1.10 x 0.55m. At the foot of the shaft on the north side
a round-headed doorway, rebated and with hinge-pins, opens
to the interior; there are toe-holds on opposite walls of the
shaft. Thirteenth century.
(de Caumont 1841: 325–7; Richard 1881: 263)

CHATEAU-LARCHER   **19km S of Poitiers N10 D742**
The *lanterne des morts* stands in the cemetery, south-west of
the castle and the church, above an elbow of the river Clouère.
It rises from a rectangular plinth on a three-stepped semicircular base, a cylindrical shaft surrounded at the foot by a flat-
tened torus linked by claws to the angles of the plinth; overall
height 5.70m, diameter 1.00m. The four oriented lantern
windows are round-headed, with an outward splay, beneath a

Antigny (Vienne)

Château-Larcher (Vienne)

roll-cornice and a conical roof carved in a serrated pattern and surmounted by a nineteenth-century Maltese cross. On the west side a rectangular stone table is corbelled out from the top of the plinth, and on the north a rectangular doorway 0.65 x 0.35m opens into the foot of the shaft, whose cavity provides no climbing notches. Thirteenth century.
(Mauduyt 1838: 51–3)

CIVAUX   32km SE of Poitiers N147 D83

The small low window, now walled up, in the east wall of the ruined fifteenth-century chapel of this early Christian necropolis is thought to have held a funerary lamp.
(Ginot 1926: 321)

JOURNET   9km E of Montmorillon D727 D121

Until 1980 this *lanterne des morts* stood at the side of a street leading out from the village square (once the cemetery). In that year it was dismantled and rebuilt in an open space on the north-east side of the village. It stands on a cubical plinth on a rectangular platform approached by four (originally seven) steps on the west side. The lantern chamber stands on a cylindrical shaft, height overall 5.50m diameter 0.9m. It is simply formed, of four curved rectangular slabs standing vertically between string courses, widely spaced and with the edges internally chamfered. A Maltese cross crowns the conical roof. A full-width stone table supported by a slender pillar projects westward from the top of the plinth. Adjacent to it, facing south-west, is a round-headed doorway to the shaft, 0.65m x 0.30m, only large enough to admit a child; spirally placed footholds are cut in the shaft wall. Twelfth century.
(Cousseau 1843)

Lanterns for the Dead

Civaux (Vienne): east end of the cemetery chapel

Journet (Vienne)

PLAISANCE-SUR-GARTEMPE
12km S of Montmorillon D5

In the cemetery beside the cross-roads in the village. Only the lower part of this square *lanterne des morts* still survives, much disturbed and leaning. The remnants consist of a rectangular plinth on a circular three-stepped base supporting on the north side a piece of the wall of the hollow shaft, including two adjacent sides of a rebated doorway. Beneath the base a capacious subterranean vault, presumably an ossuary, can be seen.

(Crozet 1951: 684)

MONTAZAIS
56km S of Poitiers

Known only from an account in the cartulary of the former priory of Montazais describing the gift to the monastery by Dame Noue, wife of Gérard Tuebo and mother of Pierre Jouscerant, of three prévendiers *(about 480 pounds weight) of wheat annually for the upkeep of the lamp on the cemetery cross at the monastery.*

(du Dorat quoted by de Chasteigner 1843: 286–7)

MONTMORILLON
55km SE of Poitiers

The twelfth-century octagonal funerary chapel that stands on the south side of the courtyard of the Maison-Dieu *is known to have had a lantern over the apex of the vault; the oculus that opened into it is still present. The lantern was destroyed in 1748.*

The chapel, the octagon of Montmorillon, was the cemetery chapel of the Maison-Dieu, *a hospital founded in about 1107 and maintained under the aegis of the knights hospitallers of the order of St. John for the care of pilgrims and the sick. It has two storeys, the chapel itself and a domed subterranean ossuary, connected to it by a staircase in the wall. It is closed to the public pending restoration.*

(Lambert 1954: 125–9)

Plaisance-sur-Gartempe (Vienne)

SAINT-LÉOMER   9km E of Montmorillon

A square lantern-tower, 6.0m high, with a small arched door-way and a stone table; it was destroyed in 1875 in the course of road-building.
(de Chasteigner 1843: 303; Crozet 1951: 684)

Charente-Maritime

AULNAY   17km NE of Saint-Jean d'Angély D950

The paired lantern-turrets surmounting the massive buttresses on either side of the west front of the twelfth-century church of Saint-Pierre de la Tour are reached by spiral staircases and each has the means of suspending a lantern. Aulnay was an important stage on the road to Compostela, and these lanterns were primarily intended for the guidance and welcoming of pilgrims. But as they also overlook the cemetery, it is thought that they may from time to time have served as *lanternes des morts*.
(Chagnolleau 1938: 46)

FENIOUX   8.5km W of Saint-Jean d'Angély D127

The impressive appearance of this great lantern owes much to its solitary position in the silence of the remote wooded valley that it dominates. A hundred metres to the east, the west front of its twelfth-century church offers a majestic display of narrative sculpture that is among the finest of its kind in western France. The lantern stands in the abandoned cemetery, on a terrace in the hillside west of the church. Eleven limestone columns are conjoined to form a massive hollow pillar supporting the lantern; they stand, with one exception, in pairs on segmental slabs surrounded by a basal torus, on a square stone plinth that is partly buried in the slope of the hill. The capitals are decorated with acanthus forming a continuous band below the circular cornice on which the lantern

Aulnay (Charente-Maritime): lantern-turret over the south-west corner of the church of Saint-Pierre de la Tour

Fenioux (Charente-Maritime): east aspect

Fenioux: the lantern-chamber, east face

stands. The lantern is formed of thirteen short colonnettes with square bases and capitals, spaced out to allow passage of the light; with three exceptions these are alternately *fortes et faibles*. Internally each is engaged into a vertical member of square section that contributes to the support of the four-sided pyramidal roof which, with its stone cross, appears top-heavy; it is built up of courses of stone carved with down-pointing scales and has in the east face a small lattice window whose purpose is unexplained. In the centre of each face of the roof the upper cornice carries a ball-finial; the ball on the south face is damaged and was at one time mistaken for a crescent.

Beneath the plinth, on the south side, a narrow passage flanked by stepped walls leads in to the foot of an internal spiral stair of thirty-four steps to the lantern chamber. A holy-water stoup has been excavated in the upper surface of the plinth at its south-west corner.

The appearance of the lantern chamber differs in certain respects from early nineteenth-century descriptions and illustrations, in which the damaged ball-finial is the only one shown, and the small pillars appear as square in section. These alterations are unrecorded; they may have been carried out at the time of the restoration of the church at the end of the nineteenth century.

Adjacent on the west side are the ruins of a tunnel-vaulted funerary chamber. A sarcophagus stands on the north side.

Nothing is known of the community that built the church and *lanterne des morts* in the twelfth century, and all trace of them has vanished. The country round is thinly populated with scattered farm buildings and houses of no great age; excavations in the valley below have revealed signs of extensive occupation, but of no later than Gallo-Roman times.
(Moreau, N., MS unpublished in Bibliothèque municipale, Saintes; Connoué 1957: 74; Eygun F: 1956: 314–15)

SAINT-PIERRE D'OLÉRON   45km W of Rochefort D723
D123 D26

At twenty metres, the highest of all the *lanternes des morts*. It soars above what was once the town cemetery but is now a car park, on a shrub-covered mound. An octagonal tower of limestone, having sevenfold roll and fillet mouldings at the angles, rising to capitals supporting the imposts of a blind arcade of pointed arches encircling the tower below the lantern. This is hexagonal, with sides set back behind the cornice of the tower; its tall round-headed windows have hood-moulds and cylindrical jamb-shafts. The hexagonal spirelet with a single roll at the angles is said to be an eighteenth-century replacement for an earlier conical spire which was struck by lightning.

A massive stone table stands at the foot of the west face; above it, at mid-height of the shaft, a dripstone strip, turned down at the sides, is presumably intended to deflect rain-water from the table. On the north-east face a doorway, raised two metres above the base, leads to the spiral stairway by which the lantern is reached. An inscribed slab lying at the foot of the west face declares the monument to be of the twelfth century, but most authors regard it as of the thirteenth century at the earliest.

(Moreau 1840: 331; Connoué 1955: 111)

Saint-Pierre d'Oléron (Charente-Maritime)

Saint-Pierre d'Oléron: the lantern chamber

Charente

ANGOULÊME
There was at one time a twelfth-century *lanterne des morts* in what was known as the 'little cemetery' on the north side of the formerly Romanesque church of Saint-André. In the course of several rebuildings that the church underwent, most of the lantern-tower disappeared, part of it surviving as the chimney-stalk of a neighbouring house. During clearance of the site in the present century, a section of the shaft was preserved and mounted on a pedestal at the east end of the church. It is a cylinder 2.00m high, 1.05m diameter, the lower half decorated with parallel serrated bands. The upper half is a plain truncated cone with an encircling band above and below; above the lower band the lowest course of stone is pierced by a diametrically opposed pair of square openings. Hardly adequate as lantern openings, their purpose is not clear.
(George 1899: 86–7)

BRIGUEUIL   **19km SE of Confolens D30**
The remains of the *lanterne des morts* stand in the cemetery. They consist of the base, part of the shaft and a cross. The cylindrical shaft, 2.40m x 0.64m, stands on a square base; it has been cleanly decapitated, and the resulting opening is stopped by a truncated cone, decorated above and below with tori, that bears a cross whose massive proportions suggest it originally belonged elsewhere. At the foot of the shaft, facing south, is a rebated opening 0.48m x 0.25m; inside, the smooth wall of what remains of the shaft is notched for climbing. The large block of stone adjacent on the east is a memorial to a former curé and is unrelated to the *lanterne des morts*.
(George 1933: 49)

Angoulême (Charente): remains of the lantern of the church of
Saint-André

Brigueuil (Charente)

CELLEFROUIN 29km SW of Confolens D951 D739

The *lanterne des morts* stands in the cliff-top cemetery high above the village and the abbey church of its former Augustinian monastery. It is a polygonal tower 12.50m high that forms a conspicuous landmark on the approach from the north. The shaft is made up of eight conjoined columns enclosing a narrow central cavity; they stand on a massive, square, pilastered plinth on a wide circular base of five steps. Four columns face the cardinal points and are of larger diameter than those intervening. A torus surrounding the foot of each column is linked to the corresponding angle of the plinth by a massive claw. The plain concave capitals support a conical roof made up of diminishing courses of stone carved in an inverted saw-tooth pattern; the topmost course supports an orb. The lowest course is interrupted by the four very small rectangular lantern openings directed on the cardinal points. A fifth opening above and facing north-east may have been intended to give access to the pulley by which the lamp was raised.

The column facing north is interrupted 3.00m above the base by an opening 0.40m square through which the lamp would have been inserted into the extremely narrow shaft. The curve of the capitals and the presence of claws at the angles of the plinth indicate a late twelfth-century origin. (Bequet 1932: 81–90)

PRANZAC 17km E of Angoulême D699

In the former cemetery on the west side of the village, surrounded till recently by a grove of elms. A plain cylindrical limestone column 6.50m high, 1.00m in diameter, rising from a flat square plinth on a wide circular base of six steps. Four rectangular lantern openings with outwardly splayed sides face the cardinal points below a roll-cornice decorated with a row of eight-pointed stars. At three-quarter height the shaft is

pierced by two diametrically opposed oculi, a feature not found anywhere else and so far unexplained. The plain conical stone roof bears a Maltese cross. On the north side of the column a rectangular doorway with rebated sides, 0.65m x 0.40m opens to the interior, whose wall is provided with spirally disposed footholds. Below and to the left of the doorway is a recess 210 x 175mm, 100mm deep, the purpose of which is not obvious; it is much too small to be used as a credence. Twelfth century.
(de Chasteigner 1843: 302–3)

Cellefrouin (Charente)

Pranzac (Charente)

AQUITAINE

Gironde

LIBOURNE
25km E of Bordeaux N89

A cylindrical tower with a domed roof, approximately 11.00m high, 2.00m diameter, with an internal spiral stair and three tall rectangular lantern windows, engaged into the east wall of the south aisle of the church of Saint-Jean Baptiste. It has been suggested that this was originally a free-standing *lanterne des morts* of the twelfth century that became incorporated into the fabric of the church when this was extended eastwards in 1306.

(Montouroy 1967: 69–78)

SAINT-ÉMILION
6.5km E of Libourne

A beacon on the top of a high cross in the centre of the former cemetery. It was said to have been used as a landmark for funeral processions coming from a distance, and may also have served as a lanterne des morts.

(Montouroy 1967: 72)

Dordogne

ATUR
6km S of Périgueux D2

In a small enclosed meadow, once the cemetery of this hilltop village on the southern outskirts of Périgueux. A cylindrical column 6.00m high, 1.00m diameter, standing on a circular plinth with iron railings set in. On the east side a rectangular doorway 1.00m above the foot opens to the interior where, it is said, climbing notches are present. The lantern has four oriented rectangular openings, separated by upright members whose external surfaces are carved in a pattern of twin

79

Libourne (Gironde): lantern incorporated in the east wall of the church of Saint-Jean Baptiste

Atur (Dordogne)

conjoined columns with simple capitals. There is no cornice; the column is stopped by a concave-sided cone rising to a pineapple finial and a modern iron cross. Twelfth century. (Vauthier 1853: 149–50)

CHERVEIX-CUBAS   35km NE of Périgueux D5

East of the church, in the cemetery of the commune of Cherveix-Cubas. A round tower of primitive appearance, built of dressed limestone blocks, 4.50m high, 0.85m diameter at its widest point, whence there is a slight taper above and below. A break of continuity between the second and third courses of stone below the lantern chamber suggests that the column has at some time been shortened. It is said that this was done for the benefit of the Fontevriste sisters whose convent was established here in the fourteenth century.

The structure lacks any ornament; there are four rectangular windows surmounted by a conical stone roof and a massive stone cross. At the foot a doorway 0.55m by 0.43m faces west. Twelfth century.
(Bernaret 1879: 410–12)

SARLAT   66km SE of Périgueux D47, D10

A cylindrical funerary chapel of two storeys surmounted by a tall, slightly convex conical roof, ensconced on a steep bank in a former cemetery behind the apse of the cathedral church of St.-Sacerdos. The lower storey, the chapel itself, has a west-facing doorway later than the rest of the building, with jamb-shafts of engaged colonnettes rising to capitals decorated with an indistinct water-leaf pattern and supporting a pointed arch with hood-mould. There are three narrow, glazed round-headed windows, with stepped embrasures inside. The interior is not accessible; it is described as being covered by a sexpartite vault whose threefold ribs spring from the capitals of six engaged columns standing on a circumferential ledge. The capitals are linked by a continuous string-course and by round-headed wall arches; the ribs converge to unite at the apex of the vault in a boss carved with the emblem of the Paschal Lamb.

The vault projects into the empty upper storey, the lamp

Cherveix-Cubas (Dordogne)

Sarlat (Dordogne)

chamber, which has four tall round-headed slit-like windows oriented on the cardinal points, and on the north-east aspect an access door. Externally a sloping corbel-table marks the division between the storeys; the roof, conical, with a slightly convex outline, is divided into four horizontal sections separated by flat bands whose inclination repeats that of the corbel-table below. The existence of a crypt beneath the chapel is a possibility that awaits investigation.

The chapel is said to have been built to commemorate a visit by St. Bernard in 1147, and his gift of bread with miraculous powers of healing. For how long it was used as a funerary chapel is not known. By the middle of the sixteenth century any such usage had evidently ceased, for in 1561 a Huguenot, one Jean del Peyrat, was clandestinely buried there. It was revived in the following century when the then Vicar-General, Armand de Gérard Latour, wrote in a letter to Dom Jean Mabillon that he had put it in order and blessed it for the celebration of Mass.

By the middle of the nineteenth century it had fallen into disrepair, and the work of restoration was entrusted to the architect Abadie who, among his first suggestions, advised that the municipality should remove from it the gunpowder store they had lodged there. Later he had to suggest that the religious community that then occupied the area should desist from their intention to wall up the west door, breaching a fresh opening on the east side in order to facilitate access for those attending their offices. Not until 1894 were Abadie's successors able to consider estimates for the work, and even then a further eleven years were to pass before restoration could begin.

(Deshoulières 1927: 281–3; Secret 1982: 12–17)

LES ANDRIVAUX   10km W of Périgueux

A one-time commandery of the order of Knights Templars; the lanterne des morts that stood in the cemetery of its tenth-century church was demolished in the first half of the nineteenth century to provide material for the building of a bridge and repairs to a well-head.
(Audierne 1851: 615)

DALON   40km E of Périgueux

Known only from gifts for the upkeep of a lamp burning by night and by day in the cemetery of this long-since-vanished Cistercian abbey:

> L'an 1187, Bernard de Radulfe de Secheira avec sa femme Aiceline et ses enfans Bernard de Radulphe et Foucauld laissèrent six livres pour entretenir une lampe dans la nuit au cimitière Dalon.

> *In the year 1187, Bernard de Radulphe de Secheira with his wife Aiceline and his sons Bernard de Radulphe and Foucauld left six pounds for the upkeep of a lamp during the night in Dalon cemetery.*

and

> ... pour rappeler à tous que l'âme survit à la destruction de son enveloppe de chair, en 1187, Guillaume de Tournon a donné six livres qu'on devait employer à entretenir, pendant la nuit, un luminaire dans le cimetière de Dalon. Or, l'abbé Gérald, touche de cette pensée pieuse, réunit immédiatement les moines en chapitre et fit décider qu'à cette somme on ajouterait annuellement le prix de six sétiers de froment afin que le luminaire brulât jour et nuit.

To remind all that the soul survives the destruction of its covering of flesh, in 1187, Guillaume de Tournon gave six pounds to be used for the upkeep during the night of a lamp in the cemetery at Dalon. Whereupon the abbot Gerald, struck by this pious thought, immediately summoned the monks in chapter, when it was decided that there should be added annually to that sum the price of six sétiers of wheat, so that the light might burn by day as well as by night.

(Bonaventure de Saint-Amable, 1685: 449; Roy-Pierrefitte 1863: 12)

SAINT-NAIXENT   9km SE of Bergerac

Mentioned as existing – without description – in the report of an ecclesiastical visitation in 1875. No further record found.

(Bernaret 1875: 546)

MIDI-PYRENÉES

Lot

MEYRAGUET
40km S of Brive N20 D43

An upright rectangular recess 0.85m high, 0.57m wide, 1.30m above ground level in a buttress embracing the north-west corner of the part-thirteenth-century church. This faced into the cemetery and is believed to have been intended to hold a funerary lamp.

(Valat 1891: 53–9)

Meyraguet (Lot)   (Valat 1891)

Limousin, with parts of adjacent regions
Approximate sites of *lanternes des morts*   existing ● lost ○
Principal towns ☐

LIMOUSIN

Corrèze

NAVES   7km N of Tulle N120

A shallow rectangular niche in the west face of a buttress embracing the north-west corner of the nave of the fourteenth-century church of Saint-Pierre. Overlooking the former cemetery, this is thought to have been intended to house a lantern.
(Poulbrière 1890: 257–8)

AYEN   23km W of Brive

This unique lantern was constructed wholly within a buttress of the fourteenth-century church, wantonly demolished in 1894. The hollow buttress, square in plan, formed the shaft of the lantern, which had four openings below a half-pyramid roof, and an access door at the foot (p. 93).
(Lecler 1882: 62–3; Rupin 1894: 351–2)

Creuse

CROCQ   25km SE of Aubusson D982 D10

The hexagonal lantern above the apse of the chapel of Notre-Dame de la Visitation in the centre of the village is, by tradition, a *lanterne des morts*. It was transferred to its present site from the south-west corner of the fifteenth-century parish church when this was demolished in the mid-nineteenth century.
(Roy-Pierrefitte 1859: 4)

Naves (Corrèze)

VUE PERSPECTIVE

COUPE.

PLAN PAR TERRE.

Ayen (Corrèze) (Rupin 1894)

Crocq (Creuse)

CROZE   15km S of Aubusson D982

Though not universally accepted as a *lanterne des morts*, the claims of this diminutive lantern are supported by long-held tradition. A slender lantern-turret, with four narrow, trefoil-headed windows, is corbelled out from the south-west corner of an oratory attached to the chapel of what was originally a commandery of Hospitallers of the order of Saint-Antoine de Viennois. The chapel was built in the twelfth century at the hamlet of Saint-Frion, 5km to the north of the present site; the oratory with its lantern-turret was added in 1450 by Bertrand de Besse, commander of the order at that time. In 1885, by which time the whole building had become ruinous, it was rescued by the Marquis de Brachet who bought the stone and rebuilt the chapel in the place where it now stands, in his park at the Château du Maslaurent at Croze.

There is no public access to it; it can be seen at a distance and with difficulty on the east side of the road from Aubusson to Ussel, 4km south of Felletin, the lantern now almost invisible beneath its ivy mantle. In the hands of a children's holiday home, its listing as *monument historique* seems powerless to prevent its final ruin, this time through neglect and vandalism, and in defiance of local efforts towards preservation. (Lacrocq 1934: 58)

FELLETIN   11km S of Aubusson N682

The lantern stands in the centre of the present cemetery, on ground rising to the west of the road from Aubusson at its entrance to the town. In common with all the surviving lanterns in the *département* of the Creuse, it is no longer in its original site. It was taken down and rebuilt here in 1877 when the former cemetery (on the hilltop opposite), in which it was originally built in the thirteenth century, was closed.

An octagonal tower of granite 8.00m high, with sides 0.45m, rising on a circular base of two steps to a plain bevel-edged cornice supporting the lantern chamber that has eight

Croze (Creuse)

Felletin (Creuse)

round-headed windows. The eight-sided pyramidal roof of stone with a small iron cross, rests on a similar cornice. On the west face a rectangular doorway 0.94m x 0.43m closed by a wooden door leads into the smooth-walled shaft. No means of climbing are provided; beneath the roof can be seen a cross-bar and pulley for the chain by which the lamp would have been raised.
(Lecler 1863: 12)

SAINT-AGNANT-DE-VERSILLAT   6km N of
                                     La Souterraine D72

This lantern originally stood in the village below, in the burial ground then surrounding the church. On the closure of that burial ground in 1869 it was taken down and reconstructed in the then new cemetery on the hillside overlooking the village from the south and a wide stretch of country around.

A hexagonal granite column 11.25m high, with sides 0.50m, on a hexagonal plinth half sunk in the sloping ground; the angles are marked by slender colonnettes that rise to capitals carved with human faces, much eroded. These mouldings reappear between the six round-headed lantern windows and continue over the pyramidal stone roof to unite beneath a weather-worn Maltese cross. A rectangular doorway 0.84m x 0.33m opens on the south-east face of the shaft, 1.00m above the foot; inside the shaft there are climbing footholds, and at the top the iron hook that supported the lamp can be seen. Late twelfth century.
(de Beaufort 1861: 356)

SAINT-GOUSSAUD   40km SW of Gueret D914 D5 D48

On open ground on the north side of this windswept hilltop village. Built of granite blocks, square in plan, 5.00m high, sides 0.70m; the angles stop-chamfered. Lantern of four narrow round-headed windows, oriented on the cardinal points, over a plain bevel-edged cornice. A full-width stone shelf projects from the west face 1.20m above the base; on the opposite face at the same level is a rectangular opening 0.50m x 0.30m into the shaft. The pyramidal stone roof carries an iron cross. Until 1811 this twelfth-century lantern stood in the cemetery beside the church, where it fell into ruin. Restoration and removal to its present site took place under curious circumstances, as told by a former curé, the Abbé Dercier (1913). At the instance of the prefect of the Creuse, the local

Saint-Agnant-de-Versillat (Creuse)

Lanterns for the Dead

Saint-Goussaud (Creuse)

council decided that in order 'to celebrate in the most solemn manner the birth and baptism of His Majesty the King of Rome, the ancient pyramid known as the lantern of Saint-Goussaud, fallen by reason of its age, should be reconstructed. Completion of the restoration was marked by a *feu de joye* with fiddlers, players of the hautbois and public dancing. Dercier also records that further repairs were carried out in 1862–3 and again in 1913.
(Lecler 1863: 12–13)

LA SOUTERRAINE   32km W of Gueret N142

The cemetery lies on the northern edge of the town, a short distance north of the church. The *lanterne des morts* stands in the centre, dwarfed by the immense blocks of topiary that line the paths leading to it. Like all the surviving lanterns in the *département* of the Creuse, it has been removed from an earlier cemetery. This took place in about 1850; the present structure is not an exact copy of the original. It is a hexagonal column 6.00m high, with sides 0.40m wide, with slender colonnettes on the arêtes extending only as far as the dripstone below the roof; in the original they reached to the apex as at Saint-Agnant-de-Versillat. The lantern has six arches, round-headed with an outward splay. At the foot on the north side is a doorway to the interior, 0.87m x 0.35m. The lantern now has an electric lamp, lit, it is said, every night.
(Lecler 1863: 13)

JARNAGES   18km E of Gueret

Described as a four-sided pyramidal structure with a lantern at the top, situated close to the cemetery. Known to have existed in the sixteenth century, the fact of its position outside rather than inside the cemetery might be thought to cast some doubt on its status as a lanterne des morts.
(Lecler 1863: 13)

La Souterraine (Creuse)

SAINT-ETIENNE-DE-FURSAC   32km W of Gueret

A simple hexagonal lantern, already in ruins when first reported in 1860.
(de Beaufort 1860: 357–8)

Haute-Vienne

COGNAC-LA-FORÊT   27km W of Limoges D79 D20 D10

At the upper end of the cemetery, on rising ground, over-looking the village from the west. A square tower 6.00m high, 0.90m wide, of smoothly dressed granite blocks, flush pointed. Colonnettes at the angles are splayed at their upper ends to support the pyramidal roof. Lantern of four round-headed windows, each slightly offset to the right of centre; their height and span appear to have been reduced at some time by stone inserts. On the east face is a square opening into the shaft, 0.46m wide, 1.25m above the square basal slab which rests directly on a grassy mound. Of the late twelfth to early thirteenth century, this monument was completely restored in 1982.
(Lecler 1863: 6)

COUSSAC-BONNEVAL   44km S of Limoges D704 D901

The former cemetery has now become a large *place* flanked by the church, the *mairie* and the *lanterne des morts*. This latter is a free-standing octagonal tower built of ragstone, unrendered, standing on a rectangular plinth 1.50m high, stepped on the west side to provide both a table and a spacious footing for the priest. Above the plinth the tower rises to a height of approximately 7.50m, with sides 0.83m wide (the door side 0.90m). The doorway, on the north-west face, 1.08m x 0.62m opens into a square-section shaft equipped with footholds for climbing. A string course intersects the shaft

Cognac-la-Forêt (Haute-Vienne)

Coussac-Bonneval (Haute-Vienne)

midway between the door lintel and the base of the lantern, which has eight narrow round-headed windows below a thimble-shaped ragstone roof. Believed to have been built originally in the twelfth century, it was rebuilt in its present form in the fourteenth, possibly as a thank-offering for deliverance from the Black Death.
(Allou 1821: 359; Lecler 1863: 6–7)

MONTROL-SÉNARD 13km S of Bellac D3 D5

In the cemetery north-east of the village is a thirteenth-
century funerary chapel dedicated to St. John the Evangelist.
It is eight metres square in plan and consists of four stout,
square pillars linked by four wide, pointed arches which have
at some time been filled in. Inside, a stone altar stands against
the east wall. The building is covered by a pitched, tiled roof
which is said to be a replacement for a stone vault which
collapsed and was never replaced. Tradition holds that this
vault supported a stone lantern of considerable size, which
was lit regularly at night by oil contributed by several neighbouring villages. Looking at the building as it now stands, it

Montrol-Sénard (Haute-Vienne): the cemetery; in the background
the funerary chapel said to have been the base of the *lanterne des
morts*; in the foreground the cemetery cross (Photograph by Yves-
Bernard Brissaud from *Les Lanternes des Morts* by Michel Plault.
Brissaud, Poitiers)

is difficult to see how it might have supported such a lantern. On the other hand, is it conceivable that the lantern, which is reputed to have been square and to have resembled that at Antigny, rose not from the chapel but from the square base that now supports the cemetery cross?
(Lecler 1863: 8–9; Lecointre 1847: 622)

ORADOUR-SAINT-GENEST 17km N of Bellac
D674 D4 bis D104

In the cemetery on the northern edge of the village. The tallest of the Limousin lanterns, a slender octagonal tower 9.00m high, with sides 0.45m, standing on a massive plinth on a square, three-stepped base. The plinth is extended on the west side to form a table 1.00m high. Above the level of the table-top, on the north and south faces, small openings into the shaft are covered by metal doors. The doorway on the north might have been wide enough to admit a very small climber, since footholds are provided; but the presence of a pulley at the top of the shaft shows that a chain was used to lift the lamp. Two white marble slabs are inserted, one above the other, into the west face of the shaft at the foot: the lower a memorial to the men of the village killed in the Franco-Prussian war; the upper slab commemorates the restoration of the monument by the Ministry of Public Works in 1902. The lantern chamber has eight round-headed windows separated by slender shafts, between a dripstone above and a string course below, beneath a steeply pitched conical roof supporting a stone cross. Twelfth century.
(Lecler 1863: 9–10)

ORADOUR-SUR-GLÂNE 22km W of Limoges N141 D9

In the village cemetery, surrounded by anguished reminders of its martyrdom in 1944, stands all that remains of a twelfth-century *lanterne des morts* that was transferred to its present site from an earlier cemetery in 1773. In the process the

lantern-chamber was damaged beyond repair and not replaced. The square shaft, 6.50m high, 1.20m wide, with roll-mouldings on the angles, ends blindly in a cornice of small leaf-crockets whose elegance gives some suggestion of the beauty of the missing lantern. Above it a roughly rounded mass of rubble and mortar supports a squat stone cross. At the foot of the shaft, on the south wall, is a round-headed doorway 0.80m x 0.30m, offset to the left, an uncommon feature seen in two other *lanternes* in the same area, at Saint-Victurnien and Cognac-la-Forêt.
(Lecler 1863: 10–11)

Oradour-sur-Glâne (Haute-Vienne)

Oradour-Saint-Genest (Haute-Vienne)

RANCON   12km E of Bellac N145 D1

A cylindrical lantern tower standing on a terrace over a steep slope leading down to the river Gartempe. Just below it is the romanesque funerary chapel dedicated to S. Sébastien. The lantern stands on a circular base on a square granite plinth and rises to a height of 5.00m, with a diameter of 1.50m. There are six narrow round-headed windows beneath a conical roof surmounted by a cinquefoil emblem. A rebated doorway 0.90m x 0.70m based 1.00m above the foot of the shaft opens to the interior on the north side; inside there are climbing footholds. The circular base has a recess cut into it on the west side, where an officiating priest would stand; perhaps it was intended to accommodate a portable credence table. The massive T-shaped stone that stands inverted beside it does not fit the space. Twelfth century.
(Allou 1821: 331; Lecler 1863: 11–12)

RAZÈS   25km N of Limoges N20

An oculus in the west wall of the south transept of the four-teenth-century church, through which the light of a lamp could shine over the cemetery outside. The cemetery has long since gone, and the window has been filled with modern stained glass, so heavily leaded as to obscure both its light and its purpose.
(Lecler 1885: 11)

SAINT-AMAND-MAGNAZEIX
                    17km SW of La Souterraine N145 D20

In the cemetery below and to the north of the village. A square lantern tower standing on a square base that has become partly buried in sand. Standing 6.50m high to the base of the cross, with sides 0.95m, it is plain and unadorned apart from cham-fering of the angles. Unusually, each of the four round-headed lantern windows is offset alternately right and left of centre. The chamfers are stopped at the foot of the tower and below

Rancon (Haute-Vienne)

Saint-Amand-Magnazeix (Haute-Vienne)

the pyramidal roof, to which the iron cross is an addition of 1842. Low down in the south wall is a doorway 0.60m x 0.33m; inside the shaft open joints, well-worn, would have provided footholds for climbers. Against the foot of the west wall three stone slabs have been fashioned into a crude table; at one end of the horizontal slab a shallow bowl has been hollowed out as a stoup. It is said that there were once walnut trees in the cemetery that provided a supply of oil for the lamp. Late twelfth to early thirteenth century.
(Lecler 1882: 17, 95)

SAINT-JUNIEN 30km WNW of Limoges N141

A massive square buttress against the north wall of the north transept of the eleventh- to twelfth-century church carries a hexagonal lantern turret that would have overlooked the former cemetery below. There is a prominent dripstone above and below the lantern chamber, whose round-headed windows have at some time been filled in to half their height. The six-sided pyramidal roof carries a ball-finial. Access to the lantern is by a spiral stair within the buttress.
(Catheu 1948: 46)

SAINT-VICTURNIEN 22km WNW of Limoges N141 D3

The square twelfth-century *lanterne des morts* stands in the cemetery beside the eastern approach to the town, looking out over ground that falls away southwards to the river Vienne. A granite tower 7.00m high overall, width 0.86m, with roll-mouldings on the angles; these rise to a plain cornice supporting the lantern chamber that has four unusually wide round-headed arches. The angles are ornamented by fine colonnettes with eroded bases and capitals extending to the imposts of the arches. Over the lantern a square slab supports the pyramidal roof, which appears to have been disturbed and carries no cross. A rectangular doorway, 0.55m x 0.38m, opens 1.00m above the foot of the north wall; it is offset to

Saint-Junien (Haute-Vienne): north transept buttress with lantern

Saint-Victurnien (Haute-Vienne)

the left (cf. Cognac-la-Forêt, Oradour-sur-Glâne). The stone base on which the tower stands forms the roof of a subterranean chamber, probably an ossuary. A stone slab with an iron lifting-ring in the ground on the north side would have provided access.

(Lecler 1863: 11)

AUREIL   **11km SE of Limoges**
Gifts for the maintenance of the cemetery lantern of this Augus-
tinian priory are recorded: in about 1150 Matthieu de Royère
gave two solidi *for the upkeep of the light which he had placed in*
the cemetery, and in 1190, Simiria, a nun of Aureil, gave for the
maintenance of the lamp one sixth of a measure of oats annually.
Nothing else is known of this lantern or of its fate.
(Lecler 1882: 16; de Senneville 1900: 158, 254–5)

AZAT-LE-RIS   **26km N of Bellac**
The existence of a lanterne des morts *here is known only from*
parish registers; the cemetery in which it stood was closed some
time in the eighteenth century.
(Pénicaut 1974: 231)

BIENNAC   **2km E of Rochechouart**
An octagonal lantern seven to eight metres high, said to be of the
thirteenth century. It had disappeared by the middle of the nine-
teenth century.
(Lecler 1863: 6)

LE CHALARD   **40km SSW of Limoges**
Known only by tradition.
(Lecler 1882: 30)

LE DORAT   **12km N of Bellac**
The existence of a lanterne des morts *here is known from the*
writings of the seventeenth-century chronicler, Robert du Dorat:
'They existed at Le Dorat, Oradour Saint-Genest and many other
places in the Limousin and the lower Marche.' He adds that
they were generally square in shape, their height was from thirty
to forty feet, and they were hollow within, 'with steps which are
of iron at each corner of the stonework, as much as to hold it
together as for climbing', with a door several feet above the ground,
'and four little windows, lengthwise and as lanterns. These

windows were formerly glazed, which was done not without reason nor in vain by our fathers of Le Dorat, for they were able to place there lighted lamps or candles.'
(du Dorat R: 1620)

GRANDMONT   25km N of Limoges
The annals of the mother-house of the Grandmontine order, established here in the twelfth century, record the presence of a lamp-bearing column in the abbey cemetery: Exemia (sic) columna supra quam olim ardebat *(A special column over which there once burned a lamp)*.
(Levesque 1662: 97)

LIMOGES
Bonaventure de Saint-Amable records in his Histoire de Saint-Martial *(1685) that the city once possessed five* lanternes des morts. *Only one is described, that in the cemetery of Saint-Michel de Pistorie, the oratory of the Black Penitents:* '… devant l'église, une pyramide faite en clocher à la pointe où dedans anciennement on mettoit des lampes allumées aux vigiles qu'on célébroit.' *(A pyramid built like a bell-tower at the top, inside which they placed lamps that were lit for the celebration of their vigils.) The date of its destruction is not known; the lanterns that stood in the cemeteries of the parishes of Saint-Cessateur, Saint-Gérald and Saint-Paul are recorded as having been destroyed in 1785 or earlier.*

The finest of all the lanternes des morts *in Limoges stood at the gate of the abbey of Saint-Martial; it was destroyed, with what remained of the abbey, by revolutionary forces in 1791.*
(Lecler 1863: 7–8)

MARVAL   28km S of Rochechouart
A funerary chapel with a lantern above it, said to date from the twelfth century and to resemble the funerary chapel at Vicq-sur-Breuilh (p. 120). Destroyed by Calvinists in 1569, it was

rebuilt in 1653, only to be destroyed, once more, during the Revolution.
(Lecler 1885: 19–20)

SAINT-BARBANT   16km NW of Bellac

An octagonal lantern-tower in the cemetery, reported in 1863 to be roofless, leaning and apparently abandoned. Its height was not known; it had sides of 0.35m with the arêtes decorated by full-length colonnettes. An elegant altar, correctly oriented and formed of a single stone projecting from the west face had on its left hand a similar stone, acting as a credence. On the opposite side to the altar a doorway 0.75m high by 0.45m wide opened to the interior. It was felt that this elegant monument might have been restored at little cost, but pleas to the administration to undertake repairs met with no response and it was allowed to disintegrate until the remains were finally cleared away in the early years of the present century.
(Lecler 1863: 5–6)

SAINT-LÉONARD-DE-NOBLAT   20km E of Limoges

A five-sided lantern-tower, said to have been about ten metres high, shown in a contemporary engraving as standing on a featureless rectangular building that contained an ossuary and two funerary chapels. The lantern was said to be the most beautiful in the diocese of Limoges, if not in the whole of France; on either side of each of its windows the angles were ornamented with niches, each containing the statue of a saint; the ball-finial that surmounted the pyramidal roof was echoed by six small pinnacles above the angles, each similarly crowned. It is thought to have been destroyed during the second half of the eighteenth century.
(Lecler 1863: 7)

Saint Léonard-de-Noblat (Haute-Vienne) (Lecler 1863)

VEYRAC   13km W of Limoges

A square lantern tower, like its near neighbours at Cognac-la-Forêt and Saint-Victurnien. It was overthrown during the Revolution.
(Lecler 1885: 21)

VICQ-SUR-BREUILH   23km S of Limoges

A square funerary chapel with a pyramidal roof surmounted by an octagonal lantern-tower. It was destroyed when the cemetery was closed in 1888. (A miniature replica stands at the top of the new cemetery on the opposite hillside.)
(Lecler 1882: 89; 1920: 808)

Vicq-sur-Breuilh (Haute-Vienne): the funerary chapel (Lecler 1882)

AUVERGNE

Allier

ESTIVAREILLES   10km N of Montluçon N141 D3

The smallest of the traditional *lanternes des morts* stands in the centre of the village, once the cemetery and now appropriately called the *Place du Lampier*. It is a cylindrical tower 3.50m high, 1.10m in diameter, standing on a circular base of two steps and built of dressed stone roughly coursed, with patches of rubble infilling. The conical roof, made up of four diminishing courses of stone blocks, overhangs the top of the shaft, where each of the three round-headed lantern openings is carved out of a single piece of stone and is widely separated from its neighbour by a single stone segment. On the east side at ground level is a door to the shaft, 1.50m high, 0.50m wide. On the opposite side a crude lectern is built into the wall; the bookplate ledge is broken off beneath. This is a feature not found in any other *lanterne des morts*.
(Pérot 1897: 172–4)

BOURBON L'ARCHAMBAULT   23km W of Moulins

Known only from its brief description as being in the form of a dome, climbed by a staircase.
(Négrier 1858: 11–14)

Cantal

MAURIAC   58km N of Aurillac N122

A *lanterne des morts* was built here in the thirteenth century in the cemetery outside the town. To ensure that the lamp burned every Saturday night, the curé of the time provided an endowment by the gift of a nearby field in 1268. Rebuilt as a

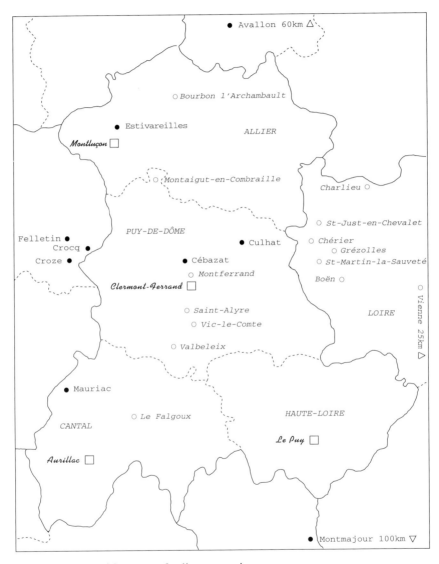

Auvergne, with parts of adjacent regions
Approximate sites of *lanternes des morts*   existing ●   lost ○
Principal towns ☐

Estivareilles (Allier)

Mauriac (Cantal)

pillar-lantern in the sixteenth century, it was reported as still standing in 1834; but at some later date it was removed to the centre of the town, where all that remains of it now is a glazed metal lantern of uncertain age standing on a pillar behind railings against the south wall of the parish church.
(Bouillet 1834: 338)

LE FALGOUX   28km SE of Mauriac
A most elaborately decorated pillar-lantern in the renaissance style, the only one of its kind in western France and similar to many of the totenleuchten *seen in Austria. Its appearance in this remote valley is inexplicable; surprising also is the fact that thirty families in the district joined together to supply oil for the lantern; on the death of one member his heir or next of kin assumed responsibility for his share. Built in the fifteenth or the sixteenth century, nothing is known of its origin, and it disappeared equally mysteriously at the end of the nineteenth century.*
(Batissier 1846: 611)

Puy-de-Dôme

CÉBAZAT   7km N of Clermont-Ferrand N9 D21
An octagonal lantern chamber 0.80m high, all but one of whose windows have been filled in, with an eight-sided pyramidal roof and a stone cross. It stands on an eight-sided pyramid that appears to rise, incongruously, from the roof of a private house. When first described (Bouillet 1846), it was considered to be a cemetery lantern; the site on which it stands was on the boundary of the former cemetery, which is known to have contained such a monument. Later it was dismissed as the chimney of a medieval kitchen (Jaloustre 1887). But a detailed examination in 1955 of the underlying building and those enclosing it showed that beneath and supporting the

Le Falgoux (Cantal) (Batissier 1846)

Cébazat (Puy-de-Dôme) (Jaloustre 1887)

pyramid are two superimposed square vaulted chambers dating from the sixteenth century, each 3.00m high and 4.00m wide, forming not a kitchen but a two-storeyed funerary chapel. Along the full width of one side of the lower chapel (at ground level) is a stone bench, believed to have been intended for the deposition of a corpse awaiting and during the funeral service in the upper chapel. First-hand evidence was found to confirm that the *lanterne des morts* was lighted on funeral occasions during the later years of the nineteenth century, long after the closure of the cemetery in 1830. (Abraham 1956)

CULHAT   28km ENE of Clermont-Ferrand N89 D493 D20
The monuments have been stripped from the abandoned cemetery on the north side of the village, where only the *lanterne des morts* remains, half-encircled by a sheltering hedge on the west side. The cylindrical column is built of smoothly dressed granite and stands on a circular plinth one metre high. On the east side a rectangular doorway 0.60m x 0.40m opens at 2.0m above ground level. Up to this level the column is solid; above it the shaft is hollow and the smooth interior is devoid of footholds. A plain bevelled cornice forms the base of the lantern chamber with its six wide round-headed windows surmounted by an encircling dripstone. The conical roof, smoothly rendered to a gentle convex curve, carries a plain iron cross. To the apex of the roof the height from the ground is 5.30m; the diameter of the shaft 1.10m. Twelfth century. (Lenoir 1869: 516–17)

MONTAIGUT-EN-COMBRAILLE
24km SE of Montluçon
A thirteenth-century lanterne des morts, *described in 1846 as standing in the centre of the cemetery, square in shape, roofed with flagstones and rather over four metres in height. It was*

Culhat (Puy-de-Dôme)

*then threatened with destruction by invasion with ivy; but when
this eventually took place is not recorded.*
(Bouillet 1874: 129)

MONTFERRAND   2km W of Clermont-Ferrand

As the illustration shows, this lanterne des morts *had many features not found in any other; the small doorway in the circular
plinth, the elaborate arcaded gallery surrounding the lantern and
bearing a circle of sculptured figures standing round the foot
of a massive crucifix. It is recorded that a one-time curé of
Montferrand had left a bequest for the maintenance of this lantern 'so that the dead might rest in peace, sheltered from the
attacks of evil spirits'. Nothing more is known of it, except for
the fact of its destruction in 1795 or 1796.*
(Tardieu 1875: 41)

VALBELEIX   36km S of Clermont-Ferrand

*A lantern first recorded in 1846, but of which no description
exists. Said to have been still standing in 1883, local enquiries
in 1980 revealed no knowledge of it.*
(Bouillet 1846: 320)

VEYRE-MONTON   18km SE of Clermont-Ferrand

In the cemetery of the church of Saint-Alyre, a lanterne des morts
*that was never described, but the destruction of which, early in
the nineteenth century, is recorded.*
(Bouillet 1846: 320)

VIC-LE-COMTE   22km SE of Clermont-Ferrand

*A circular funerary chapel 25 feet in diameter and 8 feet high,
covered by a conical roof built up of stepped courses of stone,
surmounted by an octagonal lantern-tower 10 feet high. Built
in the twelfth century, the chapel was destroyed during the second half of the nineteenth.*
(Grivaud de la Vincelle 1817: 251; Lecler 1885: 31)

FANAL OU LANTERNE DES MORTS
(Cimetière de Saint-Robert de Montferrand)
Détruit en 1795 ou 1796.

Montferrand (Puy-de-Dôme) (Tardieu 1875)

RHÔNE VALLEY

Loire

BOËN 47km S of Roanne

A lanterne des morts *was recorded here in 1839. In 1887 demolition of buildings on the site of a former burial ground revealed the remains of a square tower surmounted by a cupola, thought to be those of the lost lantern. It has to be pointed out that among these remains no sign of an actual lantern was seen. However, subsequent study of an eighteenth-century town plan showed that at the excavation site there had stood a structure described as a slender pyramid with a square window, topped by a cross. It was felt that this provided confirmation of the status of the excavated building.*
(Tailhand 1839: 433; Durand 1887: 277–85)

CHARLIEU 17km N of Roanne

The lanterne des morts *that formed the centrepiece of the funeral ceremony described by Pierre-le-Vénérable in the cemetery of the Benedictine abbey (see pp. 15–16), probably early in the twelfth century. It has never been described; its existence was confirmed in an eighteenth-century town plan. It was destroyed when the abbey was secularised in 1789.*
(Jeannez 1887: 285)

CEMETERY LANTERNS IN THE MONTS DU FOREZ

In the archives of the *département* of the Loire are records of legacies made in the fourteenth century for the maintenance of cemetery lanterns in the hilly country to the south-west of Roanne; no physical trace of them now remains. The record includes:

SAINT-JUST-EN-CHEVALET   30km W of Roanne

'Item, dat, donat et legat lampadario Sancti Justi in cimisterio dicti loci situato, pro illuminando de nocte in dicto cimisterio unum demencum siliginis semel.' *(Bequest of one measure of the finest wheat, once and for all, for the lamp in the cemetery of Saint-Just, for light at night.)*
(Testament of Jean de Cabillat, of Saint-Just, 22 September 1375)

GRÉZOLLES   48km SW of Roanne

'Item, dat et legat lampadi cimiterii de Graysolles annis singulis in perpetuum dimidiam cornutam olei.' *(Bequest of half a horn of oil for the cemetery lamp of Grézolles, every year in perpetuity.)*
(Testament of Jean Gay of Grézolles, Friday before Quinquagesima 1348)

SAINT-MARTIN-LA-SAUVETÉ   54km SW of Roanne

'Item, lampade et laterne Sancti Martini alios sex denarios Turonenses semel dedit et legavit.' *(Bequest of six further Turonian pence once and for all for the lamp and lantern of Saint-Martin.)*
(Testament of Jean Girard of Saint-Martin-de-la-Sauveté, Tuesday after Easter 1349)

Successors to these lanterns were to burn, though perhaps on a smaller scale, long after these gifts were made; in the same small area there can be found today wrought-iron cemetery crosses of the seventeenth and eighteenth centuries that bear galleries for mounting candles. An example can be seen in the church at Saint-Thurin, 15km north-west of Boën (to whose church it formerly belonged), and there are others in the neighbourhood at Saint-Didier-sous-Rochefort and at Sauvain. A much earlier example (1497) in stone stands in the churchyard at Montarcher, 40km south of Montbrison. (Chaverondier 1844: 291–2; Durand 1887: 281–3; L. Bernard, personal communication, 1982)

SAVOY AND DAUPHINÉ ALPS

Isère

VIENNE 30km S of Lyon

Until the middle of the sixteenth century there stood in the cemetery of Saint-Pierre three lions of stone, each carrying on its back a lamp on a pillar and a child, reputed to be the infant David, clinging to its mane. Legend had it that these lanterns had been miraculously transported in one night from Rome at the behest of Gregory the Great in the first year of his pontificate (590–1); they were intended to be a guarantee of salvation for all those buried in that cemetery. A lion-bearing lamp to a slightly different design was placed in each of the cemeteries of Saint-Martin and Saint-Sévère. Their ultimate fate is unknown.
(Chorier 1658; Leblanc 1879: 193–6)

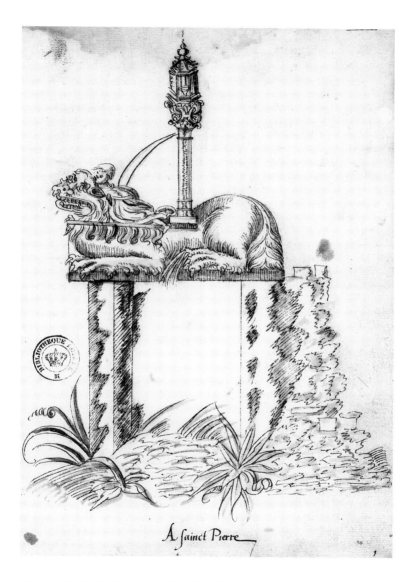

Vienne (Isère): lamp-bearing lion in the cemetery of Saint-Pierre (cliché Bibliothèque Nationale de France)

BURGUNDY

Yonne

AVALLON   52km SE of Auxerre N6

An oculus opening in a buttress on the south side of the twelfth-century façade of the church of Saint-Lazare communicates through a narrow passage with the vault over the south aisle; it is thought to have served as a *lanterne des morts* for the cemetery which formerly lay below.

(Porée 1907: 9)

Avallon (Yonne)

PROVENCE

Bouches-du-Rhône

MONTMAJOUR   **5km NE of Arles N570 D17**
The Chapelle Sainte-Croix, the cemetery chapel of the Abbey of Montmajour, stands among the remains of rock-hewn tombs a few hundred metres to the north-east of the abbey. Built at the end of the twelfth century, it is on a quatrefoil plan, with four semicircular apses radiating from a central square. It is windowless except for three small openings in the walls of the southern and eastern apses. According to Viollet-le-Duc these were intended to allow the light from a lamp suspended inside the chapel to shine over the tombs in an enclosed part of the cemetery on the south side.
(Viollet-le-Duc 1854–8: 445–7)

Montmajour (Bouches-du-Rhône)
The funerary chapel of Sainte-Croix is windowless on this side.

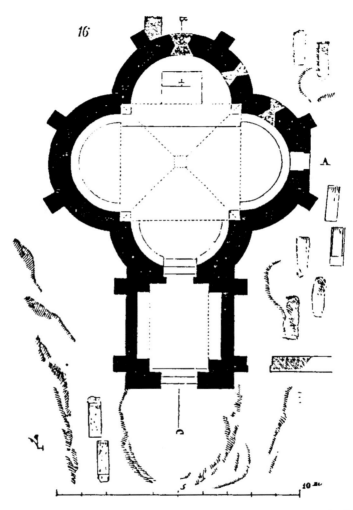

Montmajour: plan of the Chapelle Sainte-Croix at the level of the three lantern windows opening on the cemetery. The fourth opening is a doorway. (Viollet-le-Duc 1858)

Montmajour: Chapelle Sainte-Croix: the lantern windows opening on the cemetery side of the chapel

EXCLUSIONS

The architectural features by which a *lanterne des morts* may be recognised were outlined at the beginning of this work. Incorrect attributions may occur and may be perpetuated when they find their way on to maps and into guide-books. Among those that have at one time or another been erroneously considered as *lanternes des morts*, the following deserve to be mentioned.

Aigueperse (Puy-de-Dôme)
The octagonal tower engaged into the west wall of the church of Notre-Dame is a staircase tower leading to what was once a private chapel. (Deshoulières 1924)

It has to be pointed out that adjacent to that tower, at the south-west angle of the south transept, is a second staircase tower, culminating in a lantern. This, unlike the other, has never been considered as a *lanterne des morts*; a possibility that would seem to justify investigation.

Bayeux (Calvados)
The tower arising out of shop premises opposite the south-west corner of the cathedral is an ornamental chimney, of which a number of other examples once existed in the town. Similar chimneys were also to be found at Saint-Lô in the neighbouring department of the Manche, but these have disappeared. (Le Clerc 1933)

Cormery (Indre-et-Loire)
The tall column in the cemetery is a solid shaft which is not known ever to have supported a lantern.

Hérisson (Deux-Sèvres)
This monument was originally described in a guide to the history and monuments of the Gâtine district west of Parthenay,

as a lampadaire *three parts ruined (Ledain 1876: 164). However, the illustration accompanying that description shows only a group of three conjoined columns broken off a metre or two above a narrow stone base. There is no sign of a central cavity: and since there is no evidence to indicate that this column ever supported a lantern, these remains, whose total destruction was reported in 1896 (Ledain 1896: 144), would appear to be those of a* croix hosannière *only.*

Montmorillon (Vienne)

The lantern turret rising from the roof of an octagonal building to the north of the Maison-Dieu is not a *lanterne des morts*, but the chimney of a *chauffoir* erected in the priory in 1639 for the comfort of pilgrims and invalids. The 'Octagon of Montmorillon' is described on page 62.

Moussac (Vienne)

The small stone tower with a shelf projecting westward, standing in the middle of a field beside the road from Montmorillon to Bourg-Archambault, is solid, has no lantern, and is a *croix hosannière*. (Crozet 1943: 137)

Nonglard (Haute-Savoie)

Ten kilometres west of Annecy there stands at a cross-roads a solid cylindrical structure about 3.0m high, 1.60m diameter with a domed roof, below which are four equally spaced rectangular recesses. These do not communicate internally, but end blindly in the rubble-and-mortar core of the monument. Hence there is no central lamp chamber as would be found in a *lanterne des morts*. On the south-west aspect of the shaft, at mid-height is an opening 0.65m x 0.45m, in which an inclined stone slab forms a lectern. Though this monument bears a superficial resemblance to a *lanterne des morts*, and in particular to that at Estivareilles (Allier), such a designation is inappropriate since, apart from the absence of a lamp chamber, there is no evidence to suggest that there was ever a cemetery at the site on which the monument stands. In the past it was the destination of processions on Palm Sunday and for the celebration of Corpus Christi; it was probably a seventeenth-century oratory, of which, in various forms a number exist in Savoy. (Oursel 1975: 255–6; Bougoux 1989: 131)

Périers (Manche)

The hexagonal turret standing over an apse at the east end of the church is popularly believed to be a *lanterne des morts*, but Crozet (1943: 134) dismissed it as a watch-tower and, in the opinion of the departmental archivist at the present time, it is the housing for a spiral staircase giving access to the roof-space. (H. G. Duruisseau, personal communication 1989)

Saumur (Notre-Dame de Nantilly)

Attached to the south-west corner of this twelfth-century church is a subterranean funerary chapel whose vaulted roof is supported by ribs meeting in a central oculus as in the chapel of St. Catherine at Fontevraud and elsewhere. It has been claimed that this was the base of a lantern that may have been destroyed when the south aisle was added to the church in the time of Louis XI. While such a possibility certainly exists it is so far unsupported by any documentary evidence. (Verdier 1931: 27–8)

GLOSSARY

ACANTHUS Decorative motif derived from the leaf of the acanthus plant.

ANGLE-SPUR Ornamental feature, often in the form of a claw, linking the torus at the foot of a pillar to the corresponding angle of the plinth on which it stands.

ARÊTE Sharp edge formed by the meeting of two plane surfaces.

ASHLAR Smooth-faced, square-hewn building stone.

AUMBRY Wall-cupboard in the chancel of a church, intended to contain the consecrated elements of the holy sacrament.

BUTTRESS Block of masonry built against a wall as a reinforcement.

CHAMFER Bevel produced by planing off the edge of a right-angled surface.

CINQUEFOIL Decorative feature having five lobes.

COLONNETTE A slender column.

CORBEL Weight-bearing stone projecting from a wall.

CORBEL-TABLE Course of stone resting on a succession of corbels.

CORNICE Projecting feature forming the crown of a structure.

CREDENCE Small table or shelf to hold sacramental elements.

CROCKET Small ornament, usually leaf-shaped, on pinnacles and similar prominences.

DRIPSTONE Moulding over a door or window, shaped so as to throw off rain.

EMBRASURE Window- or door-opening whose sides have an inward-facing bevel.

ENGAGED Of a pillar, partly or wholly embedded in an adjacent structure.

FILLET A thin band between two mouldings.

HOOD-MOULD See dripstone.

IMPOST That part of a pillar from which an arch springs.

JAMB Side wall of a door- or window-opening.

LINTEL Structural member bridging the opening of a door or window.

OCULUS A circular window.

OSSUARY A repository for bones of the dead.

PILASTER Square or rectangular pillar engaged in a wall from which it projects to a greater or less extent.

PLINTH Rectangular course of stonework that forms the base of a column or wall.

RAG-STONE Coarse stone that breaks into small pieces.

STOUP Bowl to contain holy water.

STRING-COURSE Slender, horizontal line of stone projecting on the face of a wall.

TORUS Convex moulding of circular or semicircular profile surrounding the foot of a column.

TUFA A soft, porous limestone.

BIBLIOGRAPHY

Abraham (Mme.) 1956. La lanterne des morts de Cébazat, *Auvergne litt. et artist.* 151, 27–30.

Allou, C. N. 1821. *Description des monuments de différens âges observés dans le département de la Haute-Vienne*, Limoges.

Audierne, F. G. (Abbé) 1851. *Le Périgord Illustré*, Périgueux.

Batissier, L. 1846. *Histoire de l'art monumental dans l'antiquité et au Moyen Âge*, Paris.

Beaufort, E. de 1860–1. Recherches archéologiques dans les environs de Saint-Benoit du Sault, *Mém. soc. antiq. Ouest* 26, 356–8.

Bequet, E. 1932. La lanterne des morts et la cella de Cellefrouin. *Bull. et Mém. soc. archéol. et hist. Charente* 133, 81–90.

Bernaret, R. (Abbé) 1875. Dernière tournée pastorale dans les arrondissements de Bergerac et de Périgueux, *Ann. soc. agric. hist. et arts Dordogne* 36, 546.

Bernaret, R. (Abbé) 1879. La lanterne des morts du cimetière de Cubas, *Bull. soc. hist. archéol. Périgord* 6, 410–12.

Berthelé, J. 1889. Lanternes des morts, croix de cimetières et croix de carrefours des Deux-Sèvres, *Mém. soc. stat. Deux-Sèvres* 6, 475–99.

Bonaventure de Saint-Amable (Père) 1685. *Histoire de Saint-Martial, Apôtre des Gaules* 3, 182, 449, Limoges.

Bougoux, C. 1989. *De l'Origine des Lanternes des Morts*, Bordeaux.

Bouillet, J.-B. 1834. *Description historique et scientifique de la Haute-Auvergne*, Paris.

Bouillet, J.-B. 1846. *Statistique monumentale du Puy-de-Dôme*, Clermont-Ferrand.

Bouillet, J.-B. 1874. *Description archéologique des monuments celtiques, romains et du moyen âge du département du Puy-de-Dôme*, Clermont-Ferrand.

Boutin, E. 1975. *Prigny et ses Moustiers*, Fontenay-le-Comte.

Briquet, A. 1840. Statistique monumentale de la ville de Parthenay, *Mem. soc. stat. Deux-Sèvres* 4, 213.

Catheu, F. 1948. *La Collégiale Saint-Junien*, Paris.

Caumont, A. de. 1837. Sur des colonnes creuses ou fanaux que l'on rencontre dans quelques cimetières. *Bull. mon.* 3, 427.

Caumont, A. de. 1841. *Cours d'Antiquités Monumentales* 6, 323–47. Paris.

Chagnolleau, J. (Abbé) 1938. *Aulnay-de-Saintonge*, Grenoble.

Chasteigner, A. de (Count) 1843. Essai sur les lanternes des morts. *Bull. soc. antiq. Ouest* 10, 275–304.

Chaverondier, A. 1884. *Catalogue des Ouvrages Rélatifs au Forez ou au Département de la Loire*, 2e série, Saint Etienne.

Chorier, Nicolas 1658. *Les Recherches du Sieur Chorier sur lez Antiquitez de la Ville de Vienne*, Lyon.

Connoué, E. 1955. *Les Églises de Saintonge* 2, Saintes.

Connoué, E. 1957. *Les Églises de Saintonge* 3, Saintes.

Cousseau, J. (Abbé) 1843. Communication, *Cong. arch. Poitiers*, 539.

Crozet, R. 1936. *Lanternes des morts du Centre et de l'Ouest*, Editions de la Grand' Goule, Poitiers.

Crozet, R. 1943. *Bull. soc. antiq. Ouest*, xiii, 115–143.

Crozet, R. 1951. Communication, *Bull. soc. antiq. Ouest*, 4e série, 1, 684.

Dercier, P. (Abbé) 1913. Au sujet de fanal funeraire de St. Goussaud. *Mem. soc. sci. nat. et arch. Creuse* 19, 155.

Deshoulières, F. 1924. Aigueperse, *Cong. arch. France* 87, 165.

Deshoulières, F. 1927. Sarlat, *Cong. arch. France* 90, 281–3.

Dorat, Robert du. XVII century. Des aiguilles qui sont ès cimetières de Limousin, la Marche etc. … *ms de Dom Fontenau* xxix, 277.

Durand, V. 1887–8. La lanterne des morts et la croix avec appareil de lumières du cimetière de Boën, *Bull. Diana* 4, 277–85.

Edwards, N. 1990. *The Archeology of early medieval Ireland*, 127–8. London.

Engerand, R. 1930. Les Lanternes des Morts, *L'Illustration* 88 (4574), 281–87, Paris.

Enlart, C. 1902. *Manuel d'archéologie Française*, premier partie, 794–8, Paris.

Etoc-Demazy, F. 1841. Notice sur la lanterne des morts de Parigné l'Evêque (Sarthe), *Bull. mon. 7*, 349–53.

Expilly, J.-J. (Abbé) 1762–70. *Dictionnaire géographique, historique et politique des Gaules et de la France* 1, 44.

Eygun, F. 1956. (Fenioux). L'église paroissiale et la lanterne des morts, *Cong. arch. La Rochelle*, 304–15.

George, J. 1899. Topographie historique d'Angoulême, *Bull. et mém. soc. arch. et hist. Charente*, 6e série, 8, 86–7.

George, J. 1933. *Églises de France: Charente*, 49. Paris.

Gérard, G. de 1879. Extrait d'une lettre…à Dom Mabillon, *Bull. soc. hist. et arch. Périgord* 6, 341–4.

Ginot, E. 1926. Les Aliscamps du Poitou, *L'illustration* 167, 312.

Girouard, A. 1936. La lanterne des morts de Saumur, *Soc. let. sci. arts du Saumurois* 24, 21–3.

Hubert, E. 1889. Les lampadaires du département de l'Indre, *Rev. du Centre* 11, 109–16.

Hubert, J. 1930. Germigny-des-Prés, *Cong. arch. France* 93, 534.

Huignard, H. 1936. Congrès. archéol. Amiens, XCme session, 174.

Hula, F. 1970. *Mittelalterlichte Kultmale. Die Totenleuchte Europas*, Vienna.

Jaloustre, E. 1887. Le Château de la Malerée et la lanterne des morts, à Cébazat. *Rev. Auvergne 4*, 313–19.

Jeannez, M. 1887. La lanterne des morts de Charlieu, *Bull. Diana 4*, 285.

Lacrocq, L. 1934. *Les églises de France: Creuse*, Paris.

Lacroix, P. 1873. *Vie militaire et réligieuse au Moyen Age et à l'époque de la Renaissance*, Paris.

Lambert, E. 1954. L'architecture des Templiers, *Bull. mon.* 112, 43–4.

Lebeuf, J. 1754–8. *Histoire de la ville et de tout le diocèse de Paris* 50–1, Paris.

Leblanc, J. 1879. Transport miraculeux de trois lions de pierre de Rome dans l'abbaye de Saint-Pierre de Vienne, *Cong. Arch. France* 46, 193–6.

Lecler, A. 1863. *Les Fanaux en Limousin*, Limoges.

Lecler, A. 1882. *Étude sur les Lanternes des Morts* 1. Limoges.

Lecler, A. 1885. *Étude sur les Lanternes des Morts* 2. Limoges.

Lecler, A. 1902. *Dictionnaire Topographique du Département de la Creuse*, Limoges.

Lecler, A. 1920–26. *Dictionnaire Historique et Géographique de la Haute-Vienne*, Limoges.

Le Clerc, P. 1933. L'Abbaye de St-Lô, *Mém. soc. arch. hist. nat. Manche* 45, 16–21.

Lecointre, G. 1847. Note, *Bull. Mon.* 13, 622.

Ledain, B. 1876. *La Gâtine Historique et Monumentale*, 1st edn. Paris.

Ledain, B. 1896. *La Gâtine Historique et Monumentale*, 2nd edn. Paris.

Lenoir, A. 1867. *Statistique Monumentale de la Ville de Paris*, Paris.

Lenoir, A. 1869. Lanterne des morts à Culhat (Puy de Dôme), *Rev. des sociétés savantes* 10 (4ème série), 516–17.

Levesque, J. 1662. *Annales Ordinis Grandimontis*, Trécis.

Mabillon, J. (Dom) 1729. *Annales Ordinis Sancti Benedicti* 6, Paris.

Martin, F. 1841. Note sur la Chapelle Ste-Catherine, *Bull. mon.* 7, 540–4.

Mauduyt, L. 1838. Notice sur un monument de Château-Larcher, *Bull. soc. antiq. Ouest* 2, 51–3.

Montfaucon, B. de (Dom) 1757. Supplément au Livre de l'Antiquité Expliquée 4, 144–5 and pl.54, Paris.

Montouroy, B. 1967. Une lanterne des morts à Libourne, *Rev. hist. arch. du Libournais* 35, 69–78.

Moreau, N. 1840. Note, *Bull. mon.* 6, 331–2.

Murcier, N. 1855. *La Sépulture Chrétienne en France d'après les Monuments du xi au xvi siècles* 146, Paris.

Négrier, M. 1858–9. Les lampes ardentes dans les cimetières de Mouliherne et Montsoreau en Anjou. *Mém. soc. imp. ag. sci. arts d'Angers* 1, 11.

Oursel, R. 1975. *Art en Savoie*, Grenoble.

Pénicaut, M. (Abbé) 1974. Lanterne des morts médiévale d'Azat-le-Ris, *Bull soc. archéol. hist. Limousin* 101, 231.

Pérot, F. 1897. La lampe des morts à Estivareilles, *Bull.-rev. de la soc. Bourbonnais* 5, 172–4.

Pierre, J. 1934. Le 'lampier' d'Aigurande, *Rev. du Berry et du Centre* 26, 35–40.

Piganiol de la Force, J.-A. 1742. *Description historique de la Ville de Paris* 304, Paris.

Plault, M. 1988. *Les Lanternes des Morts*, Poitiers.

Porée, Ch. 1907. Avallon, *Cong. arch. France* 74, 9.

Port, C. 1878. *Dictionnaire de Maine-et-Loire*, Angers.

Poulbrière, J.-B. 1890. Lanternes des morts des églises de la Corrèze, *Cong. arch. France* 57, 257–8.

Richard, A. 1881. Communication, *Bull. soc. antiq. Ouest* 2, 2e. série, 263.

Roy-Pierrefitte, J.-B. (Abbé) 1859. *Notre-Dame de Crocq*, Guéret.

Roy-Pierrefitte, J.-B. (Abbé) 1863. *Études historiques sur les monastères du Limousin et de la Marche*, 12.

Rupin, E. 1894. Acte de vandalisme dans la Corrèze, *Bull. soc. sci. hist. arch. Corrèze* 16, 351–2.

Secret, J. 1982. La lanterne des morts de Sarlat, *Cong. arch. France* 187, 12–17.

de Senneville, G. 1900. Cartulaires des prieurés du'Auriel et de l'Artige, *Bull. soc. arch. Limousin* 38, 158, 254–5.

Sidoisne, A. 1931. La lanterne des morts de Bonneval, *Bull. soc. Dunoise* 15, 219–20.

Tailhand, M. 1839. Fanaux de cimetières, *Bull. mon.* 5, 433.

Tardieu, A. 1875. *Histoire de la Ville de Montferrand*, 41, Moulins.

Valat, J. 1891. La lanterne des morts de Meyraguet (Lot), *Bull. soc. hist. arch. Corrèze*, 13. 53–9.

Vauthier, E. 1853. *Le Chroniqueur du Périgord et du Limousin*, 149–50, Périgueux.

Verdier (Chanoine) 1931. Les lanternes des morts. *Soc. lett. sci. arts du Saumurois* 59, 21–31.

Verneilh, F. de 1862. Visite de la pyramide du cimetière de St-Nicolas, *Cong. arch. France* 29, 259–61.

Villegille, A. de la 1840. Notice sur des colonnes creuses ou lanternes existants au milieu d'anciens cimetières, *Bull. mon.* 6, 7–14.

Vincelle, G. de la 1817 *Monuments historiques de l'ancienne Gaule*, Paris.

Viollet-le-Duc, E. 1854–8. *Dictionnaire Raisonné de l'Architecture Française du XIe au XVIe Siècle*, Paris.

Westropp, H. M. 1863. *On the Fanaux de Cimitieres in France and the Round Towers in Ireland*, Cork.

INDEX